The Grammar Geek

An English Grammar Book for French Speakers

Ryan Fisher

The Grammar Geek – An English Grammar Book for French Speakers

Ryan Fisher

© 2018 Les Éditions JFD inc.

Catalogage avant publication de Bibliothèque et Archives nationales du Québec et Bibliothèque et Archives Canada

Ryan Fisher

The Grammar Geek – An English Grammar Book for French Speakers

ISBN 978-2-89799-003-9

1. Anglais (Langue) - Grammaires pour francophones.
2. Anglais (Langue) - Manuels pour francophones.

PE1129.F7F535 2018   428.2'441   C2018-941309-3

Éditions JFD inc.
CP 15 Succ. Rosemont
Montréal (Qc) H1X 3B6
Téléphone : 514-999-4483
Courriel : info@editionsjfd.com
www.editionsjfd.com

Tous droits réservés.

Toute reproduction, en tout ou en partie, sous quelque forme et par quelque procédé que ce soit, est interdite sans l'autorisation écrite préalable de l'éditeur.

ISBN 978-2-89799-003-9

Dépôt légal : 3e trimestre 2018
Bibliothèque et Archives nationales du Québec
Bibliothèque et Archives Canada

Imprimé au Québec, Canada

Table of contents

From the Author 5

Foreword from Denis Lacroix 7

Lesson 1: Space and Time 9

Lesson 2: The Present 15

Lesson 3: The Past 27

Lesson 4: The Future 37

Lesson 5: The Perfect 45

Lesson 6: Modals and Conditionals 57

Lesson 7: Nouns and pronouns 69

Lesson 8: Adverbs and Adjectives 81

Lesson 9: Determiners – Part 1 93

Lesson 10: Determiners – Part 2 101

Lesson 11: Prepositions 109

Lesson 12: Sentence Structure 121

Reference Section 137

From the Author

What you are about to read is a series of fictional conversations between two characters: Denis Lacroix, a student, and Paul Syme, the Grammar Geek. I hope you have as much pleasure reading these conversations as I had writing them.

Ryan Fisher
Cégep Garneau
Quebec City, Canada

Foreword from Denis Lacroix

Hello there. My name is Denis Lacroix. If you are reading this book, then you are probably enrolled in an English course at a college or a university. And, if you are like I was when I was your age, you probably do not get particularly excited when it comes to learning and studying that dreaded *g*-word. Can you guess what word I am talking about? I'll give you a hint: it has two syllables and rhymes with *hammer*. Yep, you guessed it – *grammar*. When I was a student, I always found learning grammar to be a boring, tedious task, made all the more boring by the complicated rules, confusing charts and lifeless examples in traditional grammar books. I put together this book keeping your need for something more fun and interesting in mind.

This grammar book, as you will see, is different from your typical grammar book in that it presents grammar through a dialogue between myself and a man known as the Grammar Geek. Contrary to what you might be thinking, the Grammar Geek wasn't a socially awkward, nerdy guy with glasses. His real name was Paul Syme and he was the most normal, down-to-earth person that you will ever meet. I met him back in the summer of 2010 while I was working as a waiter at the Banff Springs Hotel in Banff National Park, Alberta. I recorded our conversations with my cell phone so that I could listen to them again and again, thinking that one day I might even be able to publish them in the form of a book. Well how about that. *Le voilà!*

Like other books, it will instruct you in terms of the commonly taught grammatical forms: verbs, nouns, adjectives, determiners, pronouns, adverbs, and so on. Unlike other books, however, the goal is not only to instruct, but also to entertain. Yes, entertain! I hope that you emerge from this book having acquired a better understanding of English which will help you in your future pursuits, be them academic, professional or just personal. Perhaps maybe, just maybe, you will also emerge from these pages with a greater appreciation for English grammar and language in general.

Bonne lecture!

Denis

Lesson 1: Space and Time

> **Scene**
>
> The Windsor Lounge, 3:00 p.m. on a Sunday afternoon. I had only been working in the area for a couple of months so my English was o.k. but still a bit rough around the edges, especially my accent (which thankfully you will not be able to hear). My shift was just beginning when I approached Mr. Syme's table.

Denis: Good afternoon Sir. How are you this afternoon?

Customer: I'm great, thanks. And how about yourself?

Denis: I am doing great too, thank you. Can I offer you something to drink?

Customer: You bet you can! Something cold and frothy please. Have you got anything on special today?

Denis: Yes, in fact we have our Big Rock Scottish Heavy Ale on promotion for four dollars a pint. If you are interested in trying Alberta craft beers, that is an excellent choice.

Customer: Sounds good to me. A pint of the Scottish Heavy Ale it is.

Denis: Excellent. One ale coming up.

Customer: You know, I can't get over how gorgeous the view of the Rockies is from here inside the lounge. The pictures on the Internet are nice but not nearly as breathtaking as the real thing. You must really enjoy working here.

Denis: Yes, I really do. This is my second summer at the hotel in fact. I would like to come back next summer too. This town is a great place to work and to meet people.

Customer: And judging by the average age of the staff around here, which I'd put at about 19 or 20, I'm guessing that it's a good place to… ahem… party?

Denis: Ha. Yes, it is good for that too. Occasionally…

Customer: You know, if I didn't know better, I'd say you weren't from around here. Is that a French accent that I detect?

Denis: Yes Sir, it is. I come from *la belle province*.

Customer: Quebec! Nice. So how the devil did you end up out in Banff if you don't mind me asking?

Denis: Oh I don't mind at all, people ask me that question all the time. In fact, I just finished Cegep last spring and will be starting university in the fall. I work here to make money and improve my English. There are a lot of Quebeckers here as a matter of fact who do the same thing as me.

Customer: Well your English is already pretty advanced in my humble opinion. I think you should have said "I'm working" and "are doing" though.

Denis: Whoops. That sounds better, thanks. Actually, I am thankful for the opportunity to speak with customers like this and use English. My ultimate dream is to go to an English university to study which is why I need to improve. Plus, everybody is speaking English.

Customer: Careful there… everybody *speaks*.

Denis: Darn, there's another mistake. I feel pretty confident when I speak English but I know that I still have to look for my words and that I make mistakes from time to time. I had courses in school but I really learned English in two ways if you want the truth.

Customer: Oh yeah? Now I'm really curious. Which two ways?

Denis: The first way was by listening to music. All kinds of music: pop, punk, heavy metal, rock… everything except for country really. No matter how much I try to like it, I just can't. It just… um… how can I say it… *c'est tellement plate*!

Customer: Ha… yeah! It is pretty lame, I agree. Don't worry about offending me there… I am not much of a country fan myself. And the second?

Lesson 1: Space and Time

Denis: By watching Hockey Night in Canada! I am a BIG Montreal Canadians fan. Since coming here to live and work, I am also a fan of the Calgary Flames and Edmonton Oilers too.

Customer: Well I'll be darned. Who says rock music and hockey can't be instructive? You know, I always tell my students that you can learn little pointers in the classroom and from listening to music and watching television, but to learn a language you can't just passively absorb it: you also need to actively use it. For that reason, your decision to come here and immerse yourself in it was an excellent idea.

Denis: I agree. But hey, wait a second. Did you just say your students? Are you a teacher?

Customer: Yes, as a matter of fact I am. I teach English at the University of Manitoba. I was attending a conference in Vancouver and am on my way back home.

Denis: Is your home in Winnipeg?

Customer: Yes, it is. St. Boniface to be exact.

Denis: Wow. St. Boniface. That is a very "Franco" community... does that mean that you speak French?

Customer: *Bien oui...* or as you Quebeckers are so fond of saying, *BEN*-oui!

Denis: Ha ha. I like your accent. So I guess if I have questions then you are the man that I should ask.

Customer: They don't call me the Grammar Geek for nothing!

Denis: The Grammar Geek? That is a funny nickname. Where did you get that?

Geek: Well a couple of my colleagues who were also good friends of mine started calling me that back when I first started teaching and it has stuck ever since. I think it had something to do with my obsession with grammar: normal people watched shows like 24, Breaking Bad and the Walking Dead for the entertainment value. Not me though... I watched them to analyze the grammar. You don't get much geekier than that.

Denis: Ha ha, nope, that is definitely geeky. I guess there are worse pastimes and nicknames to have though.

Geek: Yeah. As a matter of fact, I had a rather temperamental colleague when I was teaching whom everyone referred to as the Grammar Grump. Then there was the Grammar Goon… but that's a story for another time.

Denis: Hmm. That sounds "intrigant".

Geek: Intriguing. So go ahead and shoot. What's on your mind?

Denis: Well I know that my verbs can be incorrect sometimes, like earlier for example, when I said *is speaking* instead of *speaks* and *I work* when I should have said *I'm working*. I know that sometimes I forget my 's' on words too.

Geek: You are not alone. Nouns and verbs are two areas which many English learners struggle with in fact.

Denis: Well I'm glad I am not alone. Do you have any conseil? Counsel?

Geek: Advice. Yes, I think that I do. Just remember this: nouns are, in Latin terms, *cum spatium*; that is, they represent space. Verbs are *cum tempore*: they represent time.

Denis: Spatium and tempore. I'm not sure I am following you.

Geek: Alright, let's forget the fancy Latin terms. Can you give me two beer mugs?

Denis: Okay, here you go.

Geek: Thanks. Now I'll place one of them in front of you like this. Then I'll put the other one beside it, like that. What are you looking at?

Denis: Two mugs?

Geek: Yes, you are right. You have just thought of the mugs in terms of *spatium*, or the physical space they occupy. Grammarians call that 'number'.

Denis: Number. Alright.

Geek: Now for the tempore. What is the difference between *I have a beer in the afternoon* and *I had a beer in the afternoon*?

Lesson 1: Space and Time

Denis: In the first one you mean something like "in general" or "every day". In the second one you mean that you had a beer in the afternoon yesterday.

Geek: Exactly. I just conceptualized the action of having a beer in terms of time, in this case present and past. This is what grammarians call 'tense'.

Denis: Tense. I think I learned that word in high school. Number too. I am not sure that I see how these two terms can help me however.

Geek: The notion of space and time is fundamental to language. What makes mastering English so challenging, and at times frustrating, for French speakers is the fact that the two languages express these notions differently. In French, you can pluralize words like *devoir* or *information* and say *mes devoirs* or *les informations*. However in English, we can't: we say *my homework* and *some information*, no *s*. Also, the sentence *J'étudie* can be translated as 'I study' or 'I'm studying' depending on the context. The future in English can be especially frustrating to learn due to the fact that it can be expressed in several different ways: I will go tomorrow, I am going to go tomorrow, I go tomorrow, I am going tomorrow, I will be going tomorrow, and I will have gone tomorrow.

Denis: Wow! That is a lot of different ways. Now I'm starting to see why I am so confused sometimes.

Geek: For a French speaker looking to master English, it is important to have a solid grasp of the different grammatical forms and the meanings that they evoke. English speakers like myself were fortunate to have learned these forms and meanings as young children and they remain stored up there in our unconscious minds, ready to be deployed if called upon. For us we don't even have to think about it: our language just comes out naturally.

Denis: I am thinking that it sure would be nice to have the feeling that English speakers have; the feeling where the language just comes out naturally *and* correctly.

Geek: Indeed, fluently and accurately as ESL teachers like to say. I must say that you are already a fair distance along the path to mastery in both of those departments. However if you would like me to, I could give you a hand with moving you even further along on it.

Denis: Really? That would be great. How do you propose to do that?

Geek: By doing what comes naturally to me: teaching. How does this sound for a proposal? I'm in town for the next two weeks so why don't we meet here in the lounge every afternoon, around this time, and I can give you some lessons? We can go back over some basics and delve into some more intermediate and advanced notions too. I'm actually vacationing with my wife and kids and I was planning on coming down here every afternoon for some alone time anyway. I'll confess that I am a serious beer connoisseur so having a daily rendez-vous will give me a valid reason to come and sample the beer selection in here.

Denis: That sounds like a great idea. We have a pretty wide selection so you should be able to try something new each time. And I'll be a great student, you will see.

Geek: I don't doubt it! By the way, my name is Paul Syme. What's yours?

Denis: Denis Lacroix... or that's Dennis the Cross for you English people.

Geek: Ha ha. It's nice to meet you, Mr. Cross.

Denis: Nice to meet you too Mr. Syme. Hey, I guess that you must be thirsty so I will go and get the beer that you ordered.

Geek: My beer... in all my excitement I almost forgot! You had better get to work young man.

Denis: Yes, I agree... *au boulot*!

Lesson 2: The Present

Denis: Good afternoon again, Mr. Geek. So how was your first day in the park today? Did you enjoy your sightseeing?

Geek: I sure did. We did a tour around the town, stopped in at some historical sites, gift shops and even got up close and personal with some black bears. That was fairly thrilling, not to mention a bit scary. Now I understand why so many people walk around with a canister of bear spray in their back pocket!

Denis: Yeah, fortunately we don't have to use it very often. Bears and other wildlife are a part of life here in the park and in the town sometimes… there are something like 50 different species of mammal in the area. For me it has been a great place to learn animal names: wolverine, elk, moose, bighorn and a lot more.

Geek: It's not only you… I'm learning new names too. Up until today I was unaware that there was a bird called the yellow-rumped warbler. In case you didn't know, *rump* in English is the equivalent of *fesse* in French. Who knew that there was a bird named after the color of its derriere?

Denis: Ha ha. So what are we going to talk about today? I was up late last night thinking about space and time in case you were wondering.

Geek: Judging by those bloodshot eyes of yours, you probably *were* up all night. Whether or not you were thinking about space and time, well let's just say that I have my doubts.

Denis: Heh heh. Okay, not really. But I did try out your beer mug experiment with some friends of mine. Unfortunately they weren't as impressed as I was.

Geek: I doubt they were... Actually, speaking of mugs my taste buds and I could go for something chilled right about now. I see that the Wild Rose Imperial IPA is written on your specials board so pour me one of those and we can get started talking about today's topic: the present tense. That will be a convenient place to start.

Denis: Yes, I remember you correcting me yesterday when I said "I work" and not "I'm working".

Geek: Indeed I did, so let's look more closely at these two ways of talking about the present. First there is the simple present, as in *I eat an apple, You eat an apple, He eats*, and so on. Second there is the present progressive, as in *I am eating an apple, You are eating an apple, He is eating*, et cetera[1]. One thing that I invariably need to remind my students of is the third person singular with the simple present: don't forget the s-ending and don't forget to use *does* or *doesn't* instead of *do* and *don't*. I cringe whenever a student says *He eat an apple, He don't eat an apple*, or *Do he eat an apple?*

Denis: Ouch. Please stop! I am cringing now too.

Geek: Another thing I need to remind students of is to not say things like *He drinking, He doesn't drinking* or *Do he is drinking?* They sometimes forget that there are two parts to the present progressive: the correct form of the verb *to be* and the *-ing* form. Thus in regards to the first two statements you need to say He *is* drinking and He *isn't* drinking or They *are* drinking and They *aren't* drinking, and so on. As for the third statement, the auxiliary *do* or *does* is not required in a question and so you say *Is* he drinking or *Are* they drinking?

Denis: I will have to watch myself to make sure that I don't make those mistakes in the future.

Geek: In terms of the form, another thing to watch out for is spelling. For verbs like *marry, study, pity*, or *deny* which end in a consonant and a *y*, you need to drop the *y* and change the ending to *ies* when using them in the third person singular: He mar*ies*, stud*ies*, pit*ies* and den*ies*. Watch out for these verbs when you use them in the progressive: writing (with one t), hitting (with two t's), hoping (one p), stopping (two p's), opening (one n) and beginning (two n's).

---

[1] For a complete list of the affirmative, negative and interrogative forms see the Reference Section at the end of the book.

Lesson 2: The Present

Denis: Nice to know. I have a question though: how come *writing* and *hoping* only have one *t* and one *p* but *hitting* and *stopping* have two? And how come *beginning* has two *n*'s and *opening* only has one?

Geek: Good questions. With verbs like *write* and *hope* which end in a consonant and an *e* there is no doubling of the consonant: you drop the *e* and add *ing*: *coming, using, refuting* are other examples. Whenever a verb ends in a consonant, vowel, consonant sequence, the final consonant is doubled and so you have *hitting, stopping,* and *beginning*. Other examples are *putting* and *committing*. The exception to this rule is two-syllable verbs in which the final syllable is not stressed, as is the case with *open*. We say O-pen and not o-PEN and so the consonant is not doubled. The same goes for *listen* and *happen* which are spelled *listening* and *happening*: one *n*.

Denis: That is a useful little rule. So what else do I need to know?

Geek: Well now that we have looked at some issues related to each verb's form, let's move on to look at their meanings. The million-dollar question is when do we use the simple present and when do we use the present progressive? Say, have you ever heard the joke about the three buddies?

Denis: No, I can't say that I know that one.

Geek: It goes like this: Three buddies die in a car crash and they go to heaven for an orientation. They are all asked, "When you are in your casket and friends and family are standing around you and mourning, what would you like to hear them say about you?" The first guy says, "I would like to hear them say that I was a great business leader of my time who was an example to everyone." The second guy says, "I would like to hear that I was a wonderful husband, father and teacher who touched so many lives." The last guy replies, "I would like to hear them say... Look, he's moving!"[2]

Denis: Ha! Good joke. I can just imagine the look on everybody's face. I can also see the question that is coming… why *He's moving* and not *He moves*?

Geek: You read my mind. Let's start with the simple present first. This verb form is used to express situations which are viewed as complete, unchanging, or stable over time. Situations like this include states and

---
[2] This joke can be found on the website https://jokes.cc.com.

characteristics such as *The earth is round* and *He has long hair*. They also include facts, habits, and customs as in, *Water freezes at 0 degrees*, *I do my homework every day*, and *Most Canadians celebrate Easter*.

Denis: Good so far. So what about the progressive?

Geek: The progressive is used to express situations as being incomplete or in progress at the moment of speaking. In our example *Look, he's moving*, the action is in progress at the moment the speaker says it. The subject is presented as being part of the way through the action; there is more moving to come. In other words, the action is incomplete.

Denis: I think I understand. So if I want to describe an action happening right now, I need to use the present progressive. Are there other words that go with this verb tense?

Geek: Yes. Other key words include *at the moment, currently, presently* or *these days*. Words or phrases that go with the simple present include *every day, all the time, each morning, on Sundays, whenever I get the chance*, et cetera. Another word that people typically think goes only with the simple present is *always*; however, this word can also be used with the progressive. Compare these two: *He always tells me he loves me* and *He is always telling he loves me*. One of these sentences would be used if the speaker is starting to get annoyed, and that's the second one.

Denis: Hmm. I never thought about that.

Geek: The first one has a more positive feel: *My boyfriend is so great. He always tells me he loves me. Maybe one day we'll get married!* The second one could be used like this: *There's a new guy at work and he's really creepy. He's always giving me little gifts and telling me he loves me. Should I tell the boss about it? He's really starting to get on my nerves.*

Denis: Neat. Hey, I don't know if it is true but I think I have heard people say things like "I am taking the bus for the next little while" when they are not actually on the bus when they say it. Can you explain what's going on there?

Geek: Very good observation. Let me explain it by throwing another example like it your way. If you were to ask me what I would like to drink and I said *I drink Coors Light*, what would that say about my beer drinking habits?

Lesson 2: The Present

Denis: That you *always* drink it, right?

Geek: Exactly, as in *There is only one beer for me and that's Coors Light. I don't drink anything else.* I could say *I'm drinking Coors Light* even though I am not actually engaged in it at the moment. What I mean is that usually I drink another kind of beer, say Kokanee[3], but temporarily I am drinking Coors light. Perhaps I am on a diet or it's the only thing on the menu and I'm desperate. Light beer… ugh.

Denis: Ok, I see now. So in my bus example, the person is only temporarily taking the bus. Perhaps his car had a *panne* and it is at the *garagiste* to be repaired.

Geek: It broke down and is at the mechanic's. Right you are. It is also possible to explain why it sounds strange for a student to say something like *I study Nursing at University* or *I live in an apartment* : university studies and living in an apartment are typically regarded as temporary periods in a student's life and so the simple form is not used.

Denis: I get it now. That also explains why I need to say "I'm working here for the summer".

Geek: Something else to be aware of with when using the progressive are verbs that evoke mental states, qualities or perceptions. These verbs are not typically used in the progressive: *be, have, love, see, know*, etc. We don't say *I am knowing the answer, He is having a mustache*, or *I'm loving you Mom.*[4]

Denis: I agree. Those sound very strange. But wait a minute… do you not say things like "She's having a drink" or "He's seeing a doctor"?

Geek: Yes, we do. A verb which is normally associated with a state can be used in the progressive only if it evokes an action. For example, if I say *He is being silly*, then it is like I am saying He is *acting* silly. In *I'm having supper* or *She's having a baby* the verb have means "eating" and "carrying", both action-like, not state-like. Similarly, *He's seeing someone at the moment* refers not to perception but means that the subject is dating someone.

Denis: So I could say to a girl "Your perfume smells nice" but not "Your perfume is smelling nice". Right?

---

[3] A beer brewed in British Columbia and sold throughout the Western provinces.

[4] See the Reference Section at the end of the book for a list of verbs which are state-like.

Geek: Correct. The verb *smell* can be used in the progressive only if it is being used to evoke an action. For example, you could say *Look at Uncle Albert. He is smelling the wine. He always does that before he pours himself a glass to impress his guests.*

Denis: I see.

Geek: Before we break off for today, there are a couple of other uses of the simple present which I find useful to be aware of. I see that the place is starting to fill up with customers who are probably going to be in need of your beer-pouring services so I will be brief. Suppose you are fed up with your job and you walk into the boss' office to announce your immediate resignation. Which of the following would you say: *I quit* or *I'm quitting*?

Denis: I quit!

Geek: Precisely, not *I'm quitting*. Similarly, what would you say at the conclusion of a business deal just before you sign and shake hands: *I accept* your offer or *I am accepting* your offer?

Denis: I'm accepting… no wait… I accept.

Geek: Exactly. These two situations involve what is known as performative action. A performative action is a case where the speaker performs the action described by the verb at the same time they say it. Verbs that are commonly used in this way include *refuse, nominate, promise, admit, guarantee, forbid* and *declare*. Of course, it is perfectly acceptable to say something like *I am accepting the offer* but only in reference to the future, as in *Tonight at the meeting I am accepting the offer*. We will come back to this kind of use when we discuss the future forms.

Denis: Alright. Good to know. So what is the second use that you wanted to mention?

Geek: My second use involves hockey and so you should be able to appreciate it seeing as you are a fan. If you listen closely to play-by-play announcers in hockey games, you will notice that they use the simple form: *Crosby crosses the blue line, dishes off to Malkin, Malkin dekes, he shoots, he…?*

Denis: Scores!

Geek: Yes! And not *He is scoring, Crosby is crossing*, etc. In play by play, the action happens so fast that the announcer sees all of it: nothing is incomplete about it and therefore the progressive is not used.

Denis: Well I really enjoyed our little discussion. However the lounge is really starting to fill up with customers now so I will have to leave you.

Geek: Yeah, my alone time is just about done. The wife and kids are probably wondering why I am not back yet so I should get going.

Denis: So are we going to meet again tomorrow?

Geek: Absolutely. I'll see you then.

Denis: *À demain!*

Exercises, lesson 2

Part 1: Spelling and verb forms

1. Provide the simple present and present progressive forms for each verb below. Use the pronoun in parentheses and pay attention to spelling.

    Example : marry (he)

    → He marries/He doesn't marry/Does he marry?

    → He is marrying/He isn't marrying/Is he marrying?

    a) write (you)
    b) begin (we)
    c) stop (they)
    d) mention (I)
    e) study (he)
    f) misspell (you)
    g) open (I)
    h) pity (she)
    i) hope (we)

j) spit (she)

k) shine (it)

l) enjoy (he)

m) pet (I)

2. Fill in the blank with the correct form of the verb in brackets. Choose either the simple present or the present progressive. Then make a sentence with the verb form that you did not choose.

Example: He _____ difficult today. Usually he is very friendly. (be)

- is being

- He is the president of the company and a very successful one.

a) I _____ about it at the moment. (think)

b) These flowers _____ so nice. (smell)

c) I _____ the mountains in my binoculars right now. (see)

d) She _____ like her mother. (look)

e) I _____ earlier this month to try yoga. (get up)

f) Because Marie lives in Lévis, she _____ the bridge every day to go to work. (cross)

g) We currently _____ in a tent but usually we _____ in a motel. (camp, stay)

h) How much _____ an elephant _____? (weigh)

i) Aiden _____ a summer job at the moment. He _____ as a lifeguard. (have, work)

j) This chocolate cake _____ great. _____ you _____ desserts often? (taste, make)

Part 2: Translation

Translate each sentence using the correct form of the verb in parentheses.

1. Je <u>pense</u> qu'il a raison. (think)
2. Pourquoi ton chien <u>sent</u>-il mes souliers? Arrête-le tout de suite! (smell)
3. Elle <u>sort avec</u> quelqu'un en ce moment. (see)
4. Le soleil se <u>lève</u> plus tard en hiver. (rise)
5. - Que <u>lis</u>-tu?
   - Je <u>lis</u> un article qui <u>traite</u> des effets de la musique sur l'humeur. (read, discuss)
6. Taisez-vous! J'<u>écoute</u> les nouvelles. On <u>parle</u> du débat sur l'euthanasie. (watch, talk about)
7. La route transcanadienne <u>traverse</u> le Canada. (run across)
8. - Que <u>fais</u>-tu en ce moment?
   - Je <u>pèse</u> les bananes. Elles <u>pèsent</u> deux livres. (do, weigh)
9. - Est-ce que tu <u>goûtes</u> à ma soupe?
   - Oui et je ne l'<u>aime</u> pas. Elle <u>goûte</u> le caoutchouc. (taste)
10. Je <u>prends</u> du Pepsi car je suis le conducteur désigné ce soir. D'habitude je <u>prends</u> de la bière. (have)
11. Ne le regarde pas. Il <u>fait</u> l'idiot juste pour attirer notre attention. (be silly)
12. Généralement, je <u>me couche</u> tard, mais je <u>me couche</u> plus tôt cette semaine parce que c'est la semaine des examens. (go to bed)
13. Il <u>vient</u> de Trois-Pistoles pour la rencontre de ce soir. (come)
14. Il <u>vient</u> du Nouveau-Brunswick. (come) (Note: The speaker is in New Brunswick.)
15. Ton petit frère <u>a l'air d'un clown</u>. (look foolish)

Part 3: Contexts

1. In which of the following is Frank's job only for the summer?
   a) He works at McDonald's.
   b) He is working at McDonald's.

2. In which one does Joanne usually do her homework at the cafeteria?
   a) Joanne does her homework at the library.
   b) Joanne is doing her homework at the library.

3. In which one is the baby born?
   a) Rhonda has a baby.
   b) Rhonda is having a baby.

4. In which one is the boss traveling?
   a) The boss comes from Gatineau.
   b) The boss is coming from Gatineau.

5. In which one is riding a bike only a temporary measure?
   a) Paul rides his bike to the college.
   b) Paul is riding his bike to the college.

Distinguish clearly between each of the following pairs of sentences by situating them in a context of at least 15 words each.

Example :

a) He smells it.

– Before dinner my grandfather always opens the wine, holds the cork to his nose and he smells it. He once worked in a fancy restaurant and likes to show off.

b) He is smelling it.

– Look at your hamster! You put that piece of cheese curd in his cage and he is smelling it. Do you think he'll eat it?

Lesson 2: The Present

1. a) I drink Kokanee.
   b) I am drinking Kokanee.

2. a) All employees receive training.
   b) All employees are receiving training.

3. a) They live in an apartment.
   b) They are living in an apartment.

4. a) Ms. Cole meets us every Monday.
   b) Ms. Cole is meeting us every Monday.

5. a) Kenny is a brat.
   b) Kenny is being a brat.

6. a) I see an American.
   b) I am seeing an American.

7. a) We accept the award.
   b) We are accepting the award.

8. a) He always makes jokes.
   b) He is always making jokes.

Lesson 3:
The Past

Denis: Well hello there Mr. Geek! Come right in and take a seat.

Geek: Good afternoon Denis. Thanks, I'm going to need to sit down. I spent the day riding horseback out on the trails as a matter of fact. The family and I took a ride through Bow Valley where we were also treated to a good 'ole cowboy cookout. It truly was a magnificent journey, although my backside is pretty sore right now from sitting in the saddle all day.

Denis: Poor you. Allow me to get you something to ease your pain. Seeing as you spent the day living like a cowboy, how about our Big Rock Rhine Stone *Cowboy* ale?

Geek: Big Rock. That's the popular brewery here in Alberta, isn't it? That would be great. And ask the chef to rustle me up an order of nachos. I don't know about you, but beer always makes this cowboy hungry!

Denis: Rustle? Uh… what do you mean by that?

Geek: Ha ha. I was wondering if you would get that word. That's cowboy-talk… If I say 'rustle me up some nachos' it means make me some.

Denis: Cool. I will do that. So what will be our topic of discussion today? I thought a lot about what you told me yesterday about the present verb tense.

Geek: Well I am going to tell you a cowboy joke to put us in the mood and you can guess what the topic is going to be. It came to me while I was riding today, somewhere amidst all the whining and complaining coming from my kids!

Denis: Well as the cowboys say, giddy-up.

Geek: Here goes. So there was a cowboy who rode into town and stopped at a saloon for a drink. Unfortunately, the locals always had a habit of harassing strangers, and he was one. When he finished his drink, he found his horse had been stolen so he returned to the bar, flipped out his gun and fired a shot into the air. "Which one of you sidewinders stole my horse?!?!" he yelled. No one answered so he shouted out, "Alright, I'm gonna have another beer and if my horse ain't back outside by the time I finish, I'm gonna do what I dun in Texas! And I don't like to have to do what I dun in Texas!" At that point some of the locals shifted uneasily and the man ordered another beer. After he finished it, he walked outside and his horse had been returned to the post. He saddled up and started to ride out of town. The bartender, somewhat fearful, wandered out of the bar and asked, "Say partner, before you go, what happened in Texas?" The cowboy turned back and said, "I had to walk home."[1]

Denis: Ha! Good joke.

Geek: Not bad, eh? So what did you notice about it?

Denis: Well I noticed that most of it was in the past tense so I am guessing that is today's topic?

Geek: You guessed right!

Denis: But hang on a minute. Did you say *dun*? I thought that the past tense of *do* was always *did*.

Geek: Yes, in standard English it is. What you heard was a colloquial use. If you ever travel to the Wild West, now you've got another word in your pocket.

Denis: Thanks for the advice.

Geek: Well let's go then. First of all, you need to know that like the present, the past is also expressed in two ways. First, there is the simple past, as in *I ordered, You ordered, He ordered*, and so on. Second there is the past progressive, as in *I was ordering, You were ordering, He was ordering*, et cetera.[2] In terms of the simple past, there are two things that you need to be aware of right off the bat: regular and irregular

---

[1] This joke and more can be found at the following website: https://unijokes.com

[2] For a complete list of the affirmative, negative and question forms of the simple past and past progressive, see the Reference Section.

past forms. For the regular verbs, you simply add an –*ed*: He walk*ed*, He nodd*ed*, or He chugg*ed*. Note that these are pronounced in three different ways too: a 't' sound, an 'id' sound and a 'd' sound. Try it.

Denis: Walk-t, nod-id, chugg-d.

Geek: Louder!

Denis: WALK-T, NOD-ID, CHUGG-D!

Geek: That's the spirit! I can't stress enough how important it is that you pronounce that -*ed*. It might seem like a small detail but it makes a huge difference in how you sound.

Denis: Yeah, I agree. And three ways is easy to remember, but how can I know which verbs require a 't', which require a 'd' and which require an 'id'?

Geek: The 'id' sound is the easiest to remember. You only need to use it when a verb ends in a 't' or 'd' sound, as in want-ed or need-ed. The 't' is used a more frequently, with the sounds ch, x, sh, k, f, p, s: watch-t, wax-t, wash-t, walk-t, cough-t, stop-t, pass-t. The 'd' sound is used in all other cases including vowels, b, g, j, l, m, n, r, v, and z: rowed, grabbed, waged, called, slammed, scorned, scarred, waved, and grazed.

Denis: Great. I will definitely pay attention to how I pronounce my verbs in the future.

Geek: In addition to regular verbs, you also need to know your irregular verbs like *choose* or *tell*. You don't say 'choosed' or 'telled', you say *chose* and *told*. I am sure that you studied that famous verb chart in school.

Denis: Yes, absolutely. *The* chart with the three columns that we had to memorize year after year: break broke broken, keep kept kept, put, put, put. Believe me, I am the master of those columns.

Geek: Oh you are, are you? Well then, would you like to put your money where your mouth is and try some?

Denis: No problem. Shoot!

Geek: How about *eat*?

Denis: Eat ate. Come on, give me a harder one.

Geek: Right then. How about *take* or *shake*?

Denis: Take took and shake shook. No problem there.

Geek: *Think*?

Denis: Thought.

Geek: Hmm… nice. I see that you even pronounced the 'th' correctly. How about these ones: *buy*, *bring*, *teach*, and *catch*?

Denis: Those are more difficult to pronounce but I'll try: bought, brought, taught, and caught.

Geek: Not bad. *Feel* and *fall*?

Denis: Fell and felt. Oops. I mean the other way around. You almost got me there!

Geek: Trust me, you aren't the only one that I've tripped up with those two; students mix them up often. Another mistake that I often correct is something like *I didn't wanted* it or *He didn't broke it*: you need to say I didn't <u>want</u> it or He didn't <u>break</u> it. As we saw with the present progressive, you also need to pay attention to the spelling of the *-ing* form: *writing, stopping, opening, beginning*, and so on. For these you follow the same rules that I provided when we talked about the present.

Denis: Noted. So now what about the meaning of the two forms? I mean when do I use one and when do I use the other?

Geek: Good then, let's move on to that. We say that the simple past refers to an action completed at a specific moment in the past. The word 'completed' is important here: if I say *The dog ate my homework* then the speaker means that the whole action took place. First my dear dog Newfie put the homework in his mouth, chewed it, and swallowed it: it's gone. With the present progressive, on the other hand, we say that it refers to a situation in progress, or incomplete, with respect to a certain point in the past. If I were to say *The dog was eating my homework* then I could be thinking back to yesterday when I came home, as in *Sorry Mr. Drew, but when I came into the house, Newfie was eating my homework. I managed to save a couple of pages but unfortunately he got most of it, including the assignment that was due today.*

Lesson 3: The Past

Denis: So let me check my understanding. If I am thinking back to yesterday when you came in, I could say *When you entered the lounge, I was serving some customers*.

Geek: Yes, if you mean that the serving was in progress at the moment of my entrance.

Denis: And I guess it wouldn't make sense to say *When he ran out of gas, he drove to Regina*. I would need to say *When he ran out of gas, he was driving to Regina*.

Geek: Exactly. The sequence in the first one is impossible: you can't run out of gas and then drive somewhere. It is possible, however, to run out of gas midway through a trip. You want to be careful about *when* though. Some students automatically assume that we can only use the progressive with *when* but this isn't true: *When the bomb detonated, Vincent ran for cover* or *When the bomb detonated, Vincent was running for cover* are both perfectly acceptable. In one case, the sequence is *first* the bomb detonated and *then* Vincent ran for cover. In the second, Vincent was *already* running for cover when the bomb detonated.

Denis: That is good to know. So what else should I know about the past tenses?

Geek: Well there are a few additional things that you need to be aware of. First, watch out for the expressions *Il est né* and *Il est mort*: in English we use the past tense and say *He was born* and *He died*. Second, as was the case with the present progressive, you need to be careful with verbs that have a stative sense. You don't say *The earth was being round*, *He was having a mustache*, *I was loving her*, and so on. It is only if you have an action-like sense that you can use these verbs: *Jeff was being funny*, *Jimmy was having breakfast*, *Martin was smelling the wine*, et cetera. It is actually interesting to compare how English and French treat state verbs in the past. Usually, and as you probably learned in school, the past progressive is used to translate the imparfait form and so a sentence like *Je textais ma blonde quand le policier m'a arrêté* would be translated as *I was texting my girlfriend when the police officer stopped me*. This correspondence does not exist with state verbs however and so while in French you say *Je le savais* or *Je l'aimais*, English speakers say *I knew it* or *I loved her*. Simple past.

Denis: Yes, that is interesting. So if I say in French *La bière goûtait les cerises* then I need to say *The beer tasted like cherries* and not *was tasting like cherries*, right?

Geek: Precisely. Another thing to be aware of is the expression *used to* which we use to refer to a past habit: for instance, *I used to go for a run but it was too tiring so I stopped*, or *Denise used to ride a Harley Davidson but then she switched to a Spyder*, etc. There is also the expression *was used to* which we use when referring to a situation to which we became accustomed, or habituated: *When Chris had kids, the nights were the worst. It was tough but after a while he was used to it*.

Denis: I think I see the difference. So if I say *We used to see a lot of polar bears*, then I mean that now we don't see a lot of them anymore; maybe it is the year 3000 and they have all gone extinct. But if I say *We were used to seeing a lot of polar bears*, then it means that we saw a lot of them and that after a while we did not mind.

Geek: Right. Maybe you want to say that at first you found it pretty scary to see bears wandering around the town but then you just got used to it.

Denis: I see.

Geek: The last item I would like to mention before we wrap things up for today has to do with pronunciation. We already talked about the importance of pronouncing the ed-ending. Now I would like to hear you say 'Did you'.

Denis: Did you?

Geek: Not quite. Try again, like this: Di-joo.

Denis: Dijoo?

Geek: Much better. In informal spoken English we have something called consonant linking. Because you have a consonant 'd' followed by a 'y' sound you can say dijoo, or dija which is also common. Linking also occurs with *did he*, which comes out as *diddy*, and *was he*, which comes out as *wuzzy*. Thus we often say *Diddy come?* and *Wuzzy there?*

Denis: Dija, diddy and wuzzy. Hey, you're right... anglos do say that! No wonder it can be difficult for French people to understand English people sometimes.

Geek: I totally agree. Don't worry, it goes both ways though… sometimes it is also difficult for English people to understand French speakers for the exact same reason. I mean when was the last time you said "Je… suis… allé" and not "Shwee-allé" or "Il… y… a" and not "ee-ya"?

Denis: Ha ha, you're right. I am definitely guilty.

Geek: No need to feel bad, it's just what native speakers do.

Denis: Well once again, I really learned a lot today Mr. Syme. I need to get back to work once again however… those customers over there are starting to give me strange looks.

Geek: Yeah, they look pretty thirsty. I need to get going too… I just felt my cellphone buzz me which means my wife and kids are starting to wonder where the heck I am.

Denis: Will I see you tomorrow at the same time?

Geek: Same time, same channel!

Exercises, lesson 3

Part 1: Pronunciation review

Indicate the correct pronunciation of each *-ed* form by writing /d/, /t/, or /id/. Then pronounce each one three times out loud to another student or to yourself.

spelled _____	crossed _____
smoked _____	burned _____
fainted _____	hurried _____
pointed _____	closed _____
asked _____	ended _____
danced _____	filled _____
talked _____	counted _____
entered _____	mended _____

picked _____   showed _____

parted _____   planted _____

looked _____   washed _____

lived _____   touched _____

liked _____   stopped _____

Part 2: Verb forms

Identify and correct the verb mistakes in the sentences below.

1. Fortunately, I was knowing the answer when the teacher call my name.

2. My grandmother is born in 1930 during the Great Depression. She is died last year.

3. After a few courses, I used to the intense workout and sore muscles.

4. She smelled the perfume and she thought that it was smelling great so she was buying it.

5. When I was being young I had an uncle who was visiting my family almost every day.

6. I heard a siren so I was getting out of bed and I looked out the window.

7. The alarm was sounding when the bombs began to fall.

8. My mom was used to read me a bed time story every night.

9. He is not alive anymore but my uncle Dan was coming from Texas and was having a thick American accent.

10. At the post office the clerk weighed the package and calculated the postage. Then I was paying and was leaving.

Part 3: Translation

Translate each sentence using the correct form of the verb in parentheses.

1. Quand j'<u>étais</u> jeune j'<u>avais</u> une tante qui <u>sentait</u> le tabac. (be, have, smell like)
2. Pourquoi <u>faisais</u>-tu l'idiot hier? (be)
3. Il m'en <u>a parlé</u> ce matin. (talk about)
4. Il m'en <u>parlait</u> avant la réunion. (talk about)
5. Elle <u>avait l'air</u> mieux quand je l'<u>ai vue</u>. (look, see)
6. Le professeur <u>a commencé</u> le cours quand je <u>suis entré</u> dans la salle de classe. (start, enter)
7. Le professeur <u>commençait</u> le cours quand je <u>suis entré</u> dans la salle de classe. (start, enter)
8. Mon fils <u>pesait</u> neuf livres quand il <u>est né</u>. (weigh, be born)
9. La poule <u>traversait</u> la rue lorsqu'elle <u>s'est faite frapper</u> par un camion. (cross, get hit)
10. Je lui ai dit que ton pâté chinois ne <u>goûtait</u> pas bon. C'est la raison pour laquelle il ne l'<u>a pas goûté</u>. (taste)
11. Ils <u>sortaient</u> à tous les vendredis lorsqu'ils <u>étaient</u> à l'université. (go out, be)

Part 4: Contexts

Distinguish clearly between each of the following pairs of sentences by situating them in a context of at least 15 words each.

1. a) Darren made a cake.
   b) Darren was making a cake.

2. a) Did you ride your bike?
   b) Were you riding your bike?

3. a) Kevin saw a doctor.
   b) Kevin was seeing a doctor.

4. a) I used to get up early.

    b) I was used to getting up early.

5. a) They stood when I walked in.

    b) They were standing when I walked in.

6. a) My brother was rude.

    b) My brother was being rude.

7. a) The robber fled the scene.

    b) The robber was fleeing the scene.

8. a) The cat died.

    b) The cat was dying.

9. a) We sold the house.

    b) We were selling the house.

10. a) Everyone ate one.

    b) Everyone was eating one.

Lesson 4: The Future

Geek: Well hello there Denis. Here I am again.

Denis: Hello Mr. Geek. Would you care for a beverage today?

Geek: Does the chicken have lips?

Denis: What?

Geek: Does the chicken have lips? You are probably not familiar with that expression, are you?

Denis: Uh… no, I am afraid that I am not! *Est-ce que la poule a des lèvres…* It doesn't make any sense in French. What does it mean?

Geek: It's an expression some Anglophones use from time to time. Basically, it means "yes" or "sure" or "you bet!". We have some other sayings in English that mean these things too like "Is the Pope Catholic?" or "Does a bear poop in the woods?".

Denis: Well that's good to know. If I ever get tired of saying *yes*, *sure* or *you bet* to my customers, now I know that there are different things that I can say. Thanks a lot! And here's a pint by the way.

Geek: Always a pleasure. Mmm. That's just what I needed.

Denis: So what is the *sujet du jour*? I am feeling sharp today… I got a good sleep last night. I listened to my conscience for a change and went to bed before three in the morning.

Geek: Wow. Let's get going then! So far we have looked at the past and the present so can you guess what comes next?

Denis: Hmmm… let me think about it for a second. Oh, I know… the future!

Geek: Right you are. You might recall that when we met for the first time a few days ago I told you about the different ways of expressing the future in English. I would like to go back and look at them more closely.

Denis: Yes, I remember. So I guess that we are going "Back to the Future"…?

Geek: Ha! Very well put. Are you ready?

Denis: Ready!

Geek: The two forms that I would like to focus on first are *will* and *be going to*.[1] Let's start with *will* which is used to make a prediction about the future, as in *I'm pretty sure I will graduate next year* or *I think that the summer will be a hot one*. It is also used when committing to something, or making a promise: *Yes, dear. Don't worry… I'll pick up the kids*. It can also be used when making a spontaneous, "spur of the moment" decision to do something, as in *I see you are cold. I'll close the window* or *Yeah I brought some snacks. I'll get them out of my bag for you*. I am sure that you use this type of use a lot in your line of work.

Denis: Hey, you're right. Now I understand why I say things like *I'll take that back to the chef right away* or *I'll be right back*. They are both, as you say, spur of the moment decisions.

Geek: There are two other uses of *will* that I can mention too. The first use is in requests such as *Will you pass the salt?*, *Will you come here please?* or *Will you marry me?*. The second use is in cases of refusal as in *Shucks, my car won't start* or *Nope, he won't lower his asking price*. In these latter two examples, it is like saying *My car refuses to start* or *He refuses to lower his asking price*.

Denis: Interesting. So if I say *Le camion ne veut pas démarrer* in French then in English I need to say *The truck won't start*, right?

Geek: Indeed. It would sound funny to say "My truck doesn't want to start".

Denis: Got it. So what about *be going to*? Or *gonna* as you usually say?

Geek: *Gonna* is a contracted form which is acceptable in informal speaking or writing contexts but not as acceptable in formal ones. Like *will*, *be going to* can also be used when making a prediction as in *I think I'm going to graduate this year* or *He's pretty sure the Cana-*

---

[1] See the Reference Section for a chart of the future verbs discussed in this chapter.

Lesson 4: The Future

diens are going to win the Stanley Cup. In cases where the chances are much higher that the prediction will come true, then *be going to* is used, as in *Look at those dark clouds. I think it's going to rain.* It is also used when the action is imminent and the speaker wants to convey a feeling of urgency. If I am looking up at the top shelf in the storage room and I see some big boxes that are starting to tip over, I would say *Look out! Those boxes are going to fall!* And not *will fall*. For the same reason, if you are on a boat that is sinking then you won't cry out "We will all die!"; you will say "We are all going to die!" because the chances of you dying are much higher.

Denis: Wow. Thanks for that pleasant thought. So are there any other uses I need to know?

Geek: Yes, there is one other one. *Be going to* is also used to refer to an intention or plan formed prior to the moment of speaking, as in *I have plans tonight. First I'm going to phone my Mom and then I'm going to do some laundry.*

Denis: Wow... that is *exactly* what I was planning to do. How did you guess?

Geek: So let's see then if you understand the difference between the two forms by trying a few oral exercises. What do you think?

Denis: Go for it.

Geek: Suppose someone says, "I see you have your backpacks on. Where are you going?" Fill in this blank: "We _____ hike up Bear Mountain.

Denis: Well I get the impression that the people had the intention to go hiking before the person asked them so the correct answer would be *We are going to hike*.

Geek: Good. Now imagine that a rather undesirable customer wants to complain about the temperature in the room and he blurts out, "Geez it's hot in here. Don't just stand there... do something!" You remember that the room has an air-conditioning system so after telling him to... uh... chill out, you then politely make an offer: "I _____ turn on the air conditioning."

Denis: That one seems like a spur of the moment decision and so I would say *I will turn on the air conditioning*.

Geek: Right again. Or, just *I'll*. Here's another that I'm sure you can relate to: you had a few too many… uh… let's say "beverages" and aren't feeling very well. After letting out a groaning sound, you then say "I really don't feel well at the moment. I think I _____ be sick."

Denis: There the speaker is on his way to being sick and so you need to say *I'm going to be sick.*

Geek: Good. You've got those ones down pat, or mastered, as we say. Now let's move on to some other ways of expressing the future in English. The form *will* also has a progressive form, as in *The guys will be watching the game downstairs.* We use this form to refer to a situation that will be in progress at a certain point in the future. Consequently, you could say *When you arrive, the guys will be watching the game downstairs. You can just take off your shoes and join them.* In a sentence like *When you arrive, the guys will watch the game downstairs*, the idea is that *first* you arrive, and *then* the guys will watch the game. In other words, they will wait for you.

Denis: That's clear for me now. Did you ever notice that in the first one the watching starts *before* the arriving but in the second one the watching starts after the arriving?

Geek: No, I did not but that is an excellent observation! And since we are traveling back to the future as you so cleverly put it, let's take some time to take a little trip through the present as well. Both the simple present and present progressive can be used to express the future too. There is a difference between *We visit Jasper tomorrow* and *We're visiting Jasper tomorrow*. Can you explain what it is?

Denis: I did a guided bus tour of the Rockies once and I think the tour guide said something like that when he was telling us the schedule for the day. As for the progressive, I know that I use it but I am not really sure why.

Geek: Not bad. Indeed, we use the simple present when referring to items on an itinerary or schedule that are locked in and not open to being changed: *Tomorrow we visit Jasper, then we get on the bus and drive to Lake Louise. From there we tour the area and come back home.* We use the present progressive, however, when referring to informal, more personal plans as in *Tomorrow is our day off so we're visiting Jasper. Would you like to join us? We should be back in the evening.*

Lesson 4: The Future

Denis: Got it. So is there anything else I should know about the future?

Geek: One last thing you need to know about the future before we conclude our lesson for today has to do with time clauses and how they are treated in English and in French. Let's take a French sentence like *Quand j'aurai assez d'argent, je vous paierai* which contains two verbs in the future: one in the time clause, *aurai*, and another in the condition clause, *paierai*. In English, however, we translate this sentence as *When I have enough money, I will pay you back*. That is, we use the future in the condition clause, but the simple present in the time clause. It is ungrammatical to say *When I will have enough money*.

Denis: Geez, that's good to know. I think I make that mistake sometimes. Are there other words like *when* that I should be aware of?

Geek: Yes, another word like it is *as soon as*. I will let you translate this one: *Je vous apporterai la facture aussitôt que j'aurai une minute.*

Denis: I'll bring you the bill *as soon as I have* a minute.

Geek: Exactly. And not *as soon as I'll have a minute*. You also need to watch out for the words *unless*, *before*, *after* and *until*. All of these words are incompatible with the word *will*.

Denis: Well then, thanks again for the lesson, Mr. Syme. I had no idea that the future was so… can I say "nuanced"?

Geek: Yes you can. And I am pleased that you appreciate it.

Denis: Thanks to you I *will go* to bed a wiser person tonight.

Geek: Good for you. And if you go to bed early again, I bet that wisdom *will stay* with you right up until the morning when you *will get* up.

Denis: Ahem… when I *get* up.

Geek: Just testing you *mon ami*… heh heh. See you tomorrow afternoon.

Denis: I *will* be waiting!

Exercises, lesson 4

Part 1: Will vs. Be going to

Choose the correct verb form.

1. "Could someone show me where to click on the screen? "Certainly. I **will / am going to** show you. Do you see the big red icon?"

2. "What are your plans for your vacation next week?" "We **will / are going to** spend some time at our cabin on the lake."

3. "Why are you carrying that envelope?"

    "I **will / am going to** mail it to my sister. I am on the way to the post office."

4. "Gee, it is very hot in this room."
   "You are right. I **will / am going to** open a window."

5. "I'm so sorry I can't come to your party. I have plans. I **will / am going to** study Friday night."

6. "Everybody exit the building! This bomb **will / is going to** explode!"

7. "So what **do you do / are you doing** after class today? Would you like to go for a drink with us?"
   "Thanks for the invite, but I can't. I **go / am going** to Montreal to visit my parents."

8. "Is that your cell phone buzzing?"
   "Oh yeah, it is. I **will / am going to** answer it."

9. "I can't wait! At this time tomorrow, I **will lie / will be lying** on a beach in Mexico."
   "Yeah, and I **will work / will be working** in this dreary office."

10. "Okay everyone, quiet! Matthew is here. As soon as he opens the door, everyone **will yell / will be yelling** Surprise!"

Part 2: Translation

Translate each sentence using the correct future form of the underlined verb. Use the verbs in brackets.

1. Je vous contacterai aussitôt que j'aurai les documents en main. (contact, have)
2. Quand il aura le temps, il tondra ton gazon. (have, mow)
3. Mon ordinateur ne veut pas démarrer alors je vais appeler le soutien technique ce soir. (start, call)
4. – Qu'est-ce que vous faites demain?
   – Nous partons pour Saguenay s'il ne fait pas tempête. (do, leave)
4. J'arriverai tôt. Je le promets. (arrive)
5. Lorsque nous rencontrerons des problèmes, nous vous le dirons. (encounter, tell)
6. Il arrivera quand il arrivera. (get here)
7. Voici l'itinéraire pour demain: on commence par le musée à 9h00. Après la visite guidée, on embarque dans l'autobus et on va au restaurant. (start, get on, go)
8. Annie vous fera signe au moment où vous entrerez dans la salle. (wave at, come in)
9. Je ne sais pas si Tony est dans son bureau. Je regarderai dès que j'aurai une minute. (check, get)

Part 3: Contexts

Choose the correct answer. Then write contexts for each one.

1. In which one is the speaker on an organized group tour?
    a) We visit the Empire State building tomorrow.
    b) We are visiting the Empire State building tomorrow.
2. In which one does the speaker want to know about the person's personal plans for after breakfast?
    a) What are you doing after breakfast?
    b) What do you do after breakfast?

3. In which one is the speaker trying to get the cellphone to turn on?

   a) My cellphone won't turn on.

   b) My cellphone isn't going to turn on.

4. In which one will the speaker wait for the other person's arrival before working on the assignment?

   a) We will work on the assignment when you get here.

   b) We will be working on the assignment when you get here.

5. In which one are the boxes wobbling and about to fall?

   a) Those boxes will fall on you.

   b) Those boxes are going to fall on you.

Lesson 5: The Perfect

Denis: Well look who's here once again! The famous grammar geek!

Geek: Good afternoon once again Denis. I see you are in good spirits, as usual. I trust that you got a good night's sleep again?

Denis: Yes, I did. Come over to the bar and *tire-toi une bûche*! Pull yourself a log! Is that how you say it in English?

Geek: Heh heh. No, it's not, but nice try. Pull up a chair, or a stool depending on the context.

Denis: Well pull up a stool then! And here's a pint of Sleemans, the special today. It is just what you will need to infuse your grammar powers.

Geek: Fantastic. That is just what the doctor ordered. It was a tough day at the... *ahem*... office.

Denis: More sightseeing, taking pictures and whiny kids? *Tu fais pitié*. I pity you.

Geek: Thanks for the sympathy.

Denis: So I can't wait to hear what we are going to talk about today. What is next on the list?

Geek: Well get comfortable my friend, for today we are going to discuss the verb form that I believe to be the most difficult to master for ESL learners.

Denis: And which one is that?

Geek: The present perfect.

Denis: I can't say I know what that term refers to. What is the present perfect? And... uh... is it really perfect?

Geek: Well it's not perfect in the sense of 'being without defect'. The word perfect in this sense comes from the Latin verb *perficere* which means 'to complete'. It means 'completed', a notion that we will return to in a minute.

Denis: Very well then. Let's go.

Geek: For starters, the present perfect is composed of two elements: the verb *have* plus the past participle[1]. With regular verbs, to form the past participle you simply add *-ed* and so you get *I have decided*, *She hasn't arrived*, *Have you stopped?* et cetera. What you really need to watch out for is the irregular past participles.

Denis: Aargh. The chart again!

Geek: Yes, it is coming back to haunt you. Did you not like having to drill those verbs into your memory year after year in high school?

Denis: Well, as a matter of fact, no. I get that they are important, but what I found frustrating is that we had to memorize those verbs without ever really understanding how to use them in a sentence. As I showed you a couple of days ago, however, I am the master when it comes to those verbs.

Geek: Yes, I remember. And don't worry, all of that hard work you put into memorizing those verbs was not in vain. You need to know them in order to be an accurate speaker. So let's turn to the meaning now. The present perfect is a real challenge for French speakers to master because in French you have one verb form where English has two. Take the sentence *J'ai voyagé en Espagne* for instance. This could be translated as either 'I traveled to Spain' or 'I've traveled to Spain'.

Denis: Hmm. That's interesting. My first instinct was to translate it as the simple past.

Geek: Yes, many students fall into that very same trap as a matter of fact. What you need to bear in mind is that the present perfect is, as its name states, a *present* tense. We know this because I can say 'He has finished *now*' but I can't say 'He has finished *yesterday*'.

Denis: Neat. I have never really thought of the present perfect as being a present tense before. Not that I ever really think about verb tenses though…

---

[1] For a complete verb chart, see the Reference Section.

Lesson 5: The Perfect

Geek: Ha. Lucky for you us grammarians are more than willing to devote our time to pondering questions like these! Now although we call it a present tense, it does not fall into the same lot as the simple present and present progressive. It is, rather, a special present tense: it establishes a link between a past action and a present situation. We say that it is used to focus on a present situation, or result, of a completed past action.

Denis: A present result? What do you mean by that?

Geek: Let me explain. If I say *Someone has turned off the lights* then what are we probably looking at?

Denis: Hmmm. Darkness?

Geek: Precisely. Darkness is the result of the past action of turning off the lights. What about if I say *Somebody has stolen my money*, what am I looking at?

Denis: Maybe a broken piggy bank?

Geek: Yes. Again, a broken piggy bank is the result of the past action of stealing. If I say *I see you've been down south* then what led me to say this?

Denis: Maybe the person has a sun tan?

Geek: Right again! Tanned skin is the result of being down South. So you see, with the present perfect, there is always a focus on a present situation arising from a completed past action. In my three examples, the results were a dark room, a broken piggy bank and tanned skin.

Denis: *Perficere*! I think I see what you mean. So if I say *You've finished your beer* then I'm probably looking at your empty glass, right?

Geek: Yes indeed. And by drawing my attention to the empty glass, you might, in turn, lead me to realize that I need to order another one. Which I will, if you don't mind.

Denis: What a great selling technique. Note to self… use present perfect more often!

Geek: And use it correctly. Like I mentioned at the outset, the challenge for ESL learners is learning how to distinguish between the present perfect and the simple past. What you need to remember is that while the present perfect focuses on the result, the simple past focuses strictly on an action completed in the past at a specific time. The focus is not the result but the occurrence itself and the time at which it took place: *last week, yesterday, three years ago, when I was young*, et cetera. I'd like to walk you through four different uses of the present perfect. Are you ready?

Denis: Yes yes yes! Let me get you that beer though. Here.

Geek: The first use is called the Anterior perfect, which covers the examples we have already discussed. If I walk into the kitchen and it smells great, would I say *Dad has baked a chocolate cake* or *Dad baked a chocolate cake*?

Denis: Has baked. Baking is the past action and the smell is the present result.

Geek: Right. If you were talking about the great cake that your Dad made last month, then you would use the simple past. The second use we can look at is the Experiential perfect where the focus is on the present impact of a past background or experience. Compare these two: *I've played soccer* versus *I played soccer*. In the first one, the subject is relating the fact that he has the experience: *Do you need someone to be the referee at tomorrow's soccer match? I've played soccer before so I could do it*. The second one would be used in reference to a specific time in the past, like *Last night I played soccer. Then the team went out for pizza and beer*. Do you see?

Denis: Alright, I think I get it. So if I say *I've visited Toronto* then I am focusing on the fact that I have the experience now and therefore can recommend a good place to visit or some good restaurants. On the other hand, if I am thinking of a specific trip in the past, I would use the simple past, as in *I visited Toronto last year with some friends*.

Geek: You've got it. Let's look at the third use of the present perfect now, which I call Continuative. Compare these two: *He has moved to British Columbia* and *He moved to British Columbia*. Which one would be said if the subject were now living in Manitoba?

Denis: Well definitely not the first one.

Geek: Exactly. The present perfect could be said in a context like *We won't be seeing our son for awhile as he has moved to British Columbia. He wants to find a job and improve his English*. In the second one

Lesson 5: The Perfect

with the simple past, the focus is on the when: *He moved to BC last year. He met an Australian girl though and together they went backpacking in China. She dumped him and now he's back home.*

Denis: Ha! Poor guy. So let me get this straight again. If I say a sentence like *My cell phone has died* then I am looking at a dead cell phone, as in *Oh crap. How am I going to call my girlfriend now? My cell phone has died.* If I say *My cell phone died* then I am thinking back to a past occasion: *Yesterday I was in the middle of an important phone interview and my stupid cell phone died.*

Geek: Yes, you are correct. The fourth use we can look at is the "Cumulative" use. For example, if I say *I've eaten sixteen Big Macs* versus *I ate sixteen Big Macs*, in which one am I in need of a rest before I dig into the next plate of sixteen?

Denis: Ugh. That's pretty obscene, but it would be the first one.

Geek: Right you are. It implies "so far" and means that I could eat more. In the second one, I am thinking back to last year's Big Mac eating competition of which I was the star.

Denis: Wow, I didn't know that I was in the presence of a star. May I have an autograph?

Geek: With the cumulative use, you get a slightly different nuance if you add a term like *this morning*, *this year*, or *this week*: if I were to say *I've had three cans of Red Bull this morning* then what time would it be?

Denis: Hmm. Definitely before lunch.

Geek: Right. It would be said at any time during the morning period: *No thanks, I'll pass. I've had three cans and it's only 10:00.* I could say *I had three cans of Red Bull this morning* only at the end of the morning, or in the afternoon, as in *Now I know why I'm so energized this afternoon. I had three cans of Red Bull this morning, that's why!*

Denis: Good to know.

Geek: Now an important thing to note about the cumulative use is that you often see it with the words *for* or *since* as in *I've worked here for ten years* or *since 2010*. How do the words *for* and *since* translate into French?

Denis: Depuis?

Geek: Yes. You French speakers have one word whereas in English we have two. The distinction between *since* and *for* is an important one. We use *for* for a period of time leading up to the present and *since* to refer to the point at which an action or situation began. So fill in the blank: 'I've worked here _____ 2012.'

Denis: Since.

Geek: Good. How about 'I've worked here _____ three years.'

Denis: For.

Geek: Good. Other expressions that we say include *since 2012, since last week, since I was young, since my birthday, since the beginning*, et cetera. On the other hand we say *for ten years, for two minutes, for six weeks, for five days*, et cetera.

Denis: I will definitely watch out for that from now on.

Geek: So to sum up, when you are considering whether to use the present perfect or simple past, you just have to ask yourself what kind of meaning you want to express. You can also, if it makes things easier, think in terms of the key words that I have given you. And always remember that these are BIG time no nos: *I've been to China last year, I've worked there last summer*. My ears cringe just hearing them.

Denis: Wow. Things are a lot clearer for me now. I do have one question however. When do you say things like *I've been serving* and *I had served*? Are those present perfect tenses too?

Geek: Yes, they are. I am glad that you brought them up. Those are examples of the present perfect progressive and the past perfect, respectively. The past perfect is relatively straightforward: it is used to signal that an action came before another one. If I say *When we arrived at the party, the guests had left* then this means that there were no guests; they decided not to wait for us. If I say *When we arrived at the party the guests left* then this means that we arrived, and then they left.

Denis: And the present perfect progressive?

Geek: The present perfect progressive is like the present perfect in that it also is used to focus on the present result of past action. In some cases, it does not make a significant difference which one you choose: I could say *I have worked here for 10 years* or *I have been working here for ten years* with little difference in meaning. In other cases, however, there is a significant difference in meaning which can be characterized in the same manner as that of the simple and progressive form. With the present perfect there is a notion of completeness while the present progressive carries with it a notion of incompleteness. For instance, in the sentences *He has written a book about it* and *He has been writing a book about it*, in which one is the book not ready to be read?

Denis: The second one.

Geek: Right, as in *Denis has been busy lately. He has been writing a book about his adventures in the Rocky Mountains. He plans to have it done by the end of the month*.

Denis: Ha ha. "Denis is so excited. He has written a book about his adventures in Banff and you can buy it on Amazon now."

Geek: Fine work. Now it's my turn to ask for an autograph! Now there are other cases where the meaning is slightly different. Think about these two: *The alarm has gone off* and *The alarm has been going off*. In which one is the alarm ringing?

Denis: The first one.

Geek: Correct. As in, *Darn, that's my car. The alarm has gone off. I'll be right back*. A context for the second one could be *I'm taking my car to the dealership for servicing. The alarm has been going off over the past few days and the neighbors are getting really annoyed*. Here the speaker is thinking of a series of individual occurrences, which could continue into the future if no action is taken to stop them.

Denis: So if I say *Someone has stolen my tips* then I mean that right now, my tip jar is empty. But if I say *Someone has been stealing my tips* then I mean that it has happened several times.

Geek: Exactly. And perhaps it is time for you to install a camera above your tables to catch the culprit.

Denis: Good advice. And actually, speaking of tips, if I want to have some money in my pocket for going out tonight then I need to get back to work. Those customers over there… ahem… *have been looking at me for about five minutes* so I'll have to leave you.

Geek: Ooh, very smooth! I've got to hand it to you Denis, you are a fast learner. A bit of a show-off, but a fast learner indeed.

Denis: Thank-you. I will take that as a compliment. See you tomorrow?

Geek: See you tomorrow.

Exercises, lesson 5

Part 1: The present tenses

Fill in the blank with the correct form of the verb in parentheses. Choose between the present perfect, the simple present, or the present progressive.

1. We _____ (study) French since kindergarten.
2. Mr. Whitman _____ (teach) at this school for six years.
3. I hear footsteps. I _____ (think) someone _____ (come) up the stairs.
4. My dad _____ (deposit) money in my account at the beginning of each week. He _____ (do) this until I find a full-time job.
5. I _____ (travel) to New York many times in my life. I intend to go again.
6. Every winter it _____ (snow) in Quebec and _____ (rain) in Vancouver.
7. My cousins _____ (be) in town for the past two days.
8. You _____ (make) great progress in your English skills since the beginning of the course.
9. We _____ (have) our classes in a different classroom today.
10. That man talking to Pam over there _____ (come) from Belgium.
11. I _____ (call) technical support at least ten times so far.
12. My daughters always _____ (walk) home from school every day.
13. Mr. Dukewich _____ (meet) with a client at the moment.
14. Ms. Scully _____ (parachute) five times in her life.

Lesson 5: The Perfect

15. He _____ (need) money to start his business.
16. Yuck. Something _____ (smell) awful in here.
17. Good news! You _____ (make, not) any mistakes so far.
18. Ms. Schofield _____ (change) jobs three times since last year.
19. They generally _____ (buy) all of their books from online sites.
20. Carleen _____ (study) at Laval since 2014.

Part 2: Translation

Translate the following sentences.

1. Target a fermé ses portes en 2013.
2. Apple a vendu plus de 10 millions de iPhones lors de son lancement en 2014.
3. Depuis son lancement, Apple a vendu plus de 30 millions de iPhones.
4. J'ai envoyé ma démission la semaine passée.
5. M. Burns a congédié cinq employés hier.
6. M. Burns avait congédié cinq employés avant la réunion.
7. Daryl travaille pour notre entreprise depuis trente ans.
8. Jusqu'à présent j'ai répondu à trois courriels et je réponds présentement au quatrième.
9. Cela fait cinq jours qu'Hilary est malade.
10. Cela fait deux heures que Donald joue au Xbox.
11. Mickey avait déjà terminé le travail quand je suis arrivé.
12. – Depuis combien de temps est-il ici?
    – Il est ici depuis quatre heures déjà.

Part 3: Contexts

1. In which of the following is the cat still on the roof?
   a) Tracy's cat climbed up on the roof.
   b) Tracy's cat has climbed up on the roof.

2. In which statement is Melba not practicing karate anymore?
    a) My friend Melba practiced karate for ten years.
    b) My friend Melba has practiced karate for ten years.
3. Which statement implies that the subject will write another letter?
    a) She has written three letters.
    b) She wrote three letters.
4. In which statement is the finger not bleeding anymore?
    a) I've cut my finger.
    b) I cut my finger.
5. In which one is the painting completed?
    a) I've painted your bedroom.
    b) I've been painting your bedroom.
6. In which one did the parents not wait for their daughter to arrive?
    a) When Maria got home, we made a toast.
    b) When Maria got home, we had made a toast.
7. In which one could the snake still be in its cage?
    a) Your snake has escaped from its cage.
    b) Your snake has been escaping from its cage.
8. In which statement could the subject be deceased?
    a) Brenda never played guitar.
    b) Brenda has never played guitar.

Distinguish clearly between each of the following pairs of sentences by situating them in a context of at least 15 words each.

1. a) We walked 100 miles.
   b) We have walked 100 miles.

2. a) I used Powerpoint.
   b) I have used Powerpoint.

Lesson 5: The Perfect

3. a) They lived there for 20 years.
   b) They have lived there for 20 years.

4. a) Jenny has never gone to a hockey game.
   b) Jenny never went to a hockey game.

5. a) She had dinner.
   b) She had had dinner.

6. a) I have read your book.
   b) I have been reading your book.

7. a) The teacher has marked our tests.
   b) The teacher has been marking our tests.

8. a) Someone has broken into my office.
   b) Someone has been breaking into my office.

9. a) I've been texting him.
   b) I've texted him.

10. a) Who has left the lights on?
    b) Who has been leaving the lights on?

Lesson 6:
Modals and Conditionals

Geek: Today *mon cher* Denis we are going to talk about the modals.

Denis: The modals! Awesome! So... uh... what's a modal?

Geek: Well I think we are about due for a joke, don't you think? It has been awhile since my last one and I've got a good one with a few modal uses.

Denis: Yes! A joke please!

Geek: There was a time, long ago, when sailing ships ruled the sea, and ships were always in danger of being boarded by pirates. One day, while a captain and his crew were sailing, a pirate ship sent a boarding party to try and board their ship. The crew became very worried and asked their captain, "Captain, what should we do?" but he did not seem bothered at all. "Fetch me my red shirt!" he cried out to his First Mate, who quickly fetched his red shirt which the captain put on. He led his crew into battle and defeated the pirates. Later that day, there was a cry from the lookout: there were two pirate ships this time with two boarding parties coming towards their ship. Again, a nervous crew asked their Captain, "What should we do?" and again, he was calm. "Fetch me my red shirt!" he said and once again, he led his crew to battle and won. That night, tired from all the fighting, the men were recounting the events of the day when the First Mate asked his Captain, "Captain, may I ask you why you called for your red shirt before the battle?" The Captain explained, "Well, if I am wounded in battle, the red shirt does not show the blood. It inspires the crew to continue to fight courageously and unafraid." The men were amazed and in awe of their Captain's leadership and bravery. The next day, at dawn, the lookout shouted that their ship was surrounded on all sides by pirate ships, ten in total, all with fierce boarding parties approaching. The men looked towards their captain for his usual command. One crew member cried out, "Captain, would you like me to fetch you your red shirt again?" to which the captain replied, in his usual calm tone, "No, fetch me my brown pants!!!"[1]

---

[1] This joke can be found at http://english-zone.com/esl-jokes/brown.html

Denis: Ha! Not bad.

Geek: Good one, eh? So did you get the modal examples in there? I'll give you a hint: there was one in the mate's questions.

Denis: A-ha! *Would like* and *should*. Now I remember what the modals are: would, should, could, must.

Geek: Can, could, may, might, and so on. Modals, as we will see, are very versatile. They can be used to express a number of different meanings and this is what can make them tricky little critters to master. What is essential to grasping the modals is to remember that they don't express actions in terms of reality. They are the opposite in fact: they express them in terms of non-reality.

Denis: Whoah, easy on the philosophy there, Mr. Geek. You're already starting to lose me!

Geek: Heh heh. O.k. then... Let's take an example like *I ate a taco*. Here I am expressing a real event: a taco was actually eaten, right?

Denis: Yes, it was.

Geek: The same goes for *I am eating a taco* or *I have eaten a taco*. Both of these refer to actual events in which all or part of a taco was consumed.

Denis: O.k., I follow you so far. So how do modals express non-reality as you said?

Geek: Now let's suppose I say *I can eat a taco* or *I might eat a taco*. Here I am no longer expressing a real event: I am expressing the eating in terms of capacity or possibility. In the former I am saying that I have the capacity, or ability, to eat a taco whereas in the second I am saying that eating a taco is a possibility. In neither case is the taco represented as having been consumed.

Denis: Hmm. Okay, so if I say *I must eat a taco* then I mean that it is necessary.

Geek: Precisely. Capacity, possibility, necessity, logicality, advisability... these are all different notions that the modals can be used to express.

Denis: Got it. Those are a lot of *-ty* words by the way!

Lesson 6: Modals and Conditionals

Geek: It is, I agree. Some grammarians use the term "potentialities" to refer to them all. So for starters, let's look at the modals *can* and *could*. *Can* is used to express an ability in the present, as in *Eliana can speak four languages*, or a possibility, as in *Rita can see the stage from here*. *Could* is used to express these notions but in a more hypothetical way; for example, *Eliana could speak four languages if she took courses like you* and *Rita could see the stage from here if that guy standing in front of her wasn't wearing a cowboy hat*. *Could* is also used to express these notions in the past, as in *When Martin was young, he could play classical guitar* or *Yesterday Julien could see the screen at the movie theatre, but I couldn't*.

Denis: I follow. 'I can' is pretty much 'Je peux' in French while 'I could' is either 'Je pourrais' or 'Je pouvais' depending on whether it is present or past.

Geek: Right. The modal *can* and *could* also express what is called *sporadic* possibility. Compare these two: *My boss is nasty*, *My boss can be nasty* and *My boss could be nasty*. In the first one, I mean all the time: it is a characteristic of him or her. In the second, I mean from time to time: sometimes he is nice but sometimes he is nasty; in other words, it depends on whether you talk to him in the morning or in the afternoon. In the third, perhaps I am talking about a boss I had in the past whose nastiness surfaced every once in a while, again depending on the time of day.

Denis: Good. I guess a sentence like *It can get cold here* would be like saying *Il arrive parfois qu'il fasse froid ici*.

Geek: Indeed it would... you are catching on fast once again! Another thing to note about *can* and *could* is the form *was able to*, what we call a semi-modal. We use this form in cases where the event in question actually happened. For example, does it sound alright to say *Yesterday I tried and tried and finally I could reach him on the phone?*

Denis: Hmm. I think that sounds a bit strange.

Geek: Yes, it does. Here the implication is that the subject actually reached the person on the phone and so you would need to say *I was able to* reach him.

Denis: I guess that's like saying *J'ai pu le rejoindre* then. Right?

Geek: Right again! Let's move along then and take a look at the difference between *can* and *may*. You no doubt learned in school that both can be used to express permission, one being more polite than the other.

Denis: Yes, I remember it. My teachers always insisted that I say *May I use the washroom* and not *Can I use the washroom* when I was in school.

Geek: Well I'm glad to see that someone was paying attention to instilling good manners in you! That distinction is generally true, however there are contexts in which only one way of asking for permission is possible. Compare the two sentences *May I write in pencil?* and *Can I write in pencil?*. The former is equivalent to saying "Do you give me permission" and so would be said if the speaker was addressing the teacher : *Excuse me Mr. McCarthy, but may I write my essay in pencil? I don't have my pen today*. The latter is equivalent to saying "Do I have permission" and would be used if the speaker is addressing someone who is not in a position to give permission, such as his or her classmate. In other words, *Hey Pat, did you read the instructions? Does it say anything in there about writing in pencil? Can we? I didn't bring a pen, darnit.*

Denis: Interesting. Most customers that come in here say *Can I smoke in here*. Now I see that that's because they are asking about the rules.

Geek: Yes, that is correct. Great observation. Now in addition to permission, *can* and *may* also contrast in terms of possibility. If I say *Meditation can help* and *Meditation may help*, in one of them the impression is that I have not tried it before, or I am less confident. Which one?

Denis: I vote for the second one.

Geek: Good, as in *Have you tried meditation? It may help but then again it is hard to say. Personally I've never tried it*. On the other hand, with *can* you could say *I went through stress when I was a student and I can tell you that meditation can help. It did for me.*

Denis: Is that the same thing as *Meditation might help*?

Geek: Yes, *may* and *might* are really close, although we tend to use *may* if the chances of the situation happening are slightly higher: *The coaches say that Ovechkin may play tonight* is slightly more confident than *The coaches say that Ovechkin might play tonight*. But then again, these two are *mighty* close.

Lesson 6: Modals and Conditionals

Denis: Ha ha… nice. How do you say "jeu de mot"?

Geek: The word you are looking for is *pun*.

Denis: Ha ha… nice pun. So what other modals are there?

Geek: So moving along, let's look at *should* and *must*. The modal *should* is used to express advisability, as in *You should consult a doctor* or *Should I buy a tablet?* where the person is giving and asking for advice in terms of what course of action would be the best one to take. It is also used when making an assumption about the probability of an event. For example, if you are in Quebec City and your friend left about two hours ago for Montreal then you could assert with about 60% confidence, *He should be in Montreal by now*. This sounds a bit more confident than *He might be in Montreal by now* where the chances are about 50/50. Maybe it has been an hour and forty-five minutes but you know that he is a fast driver which makes it possible for him to be in Montreal.

Denis: Got it. So what about *must*?

Geek: The modal *must* is used to express necessity, as is the semi-modal *have to*. Both of these forms convey pretty much the same message in sentences like *We were told that we must present a passport at the border* or *We were told that we have to present a passport at the airport*. Where you see a distinct difference in meaning is in negative contexts such as *You mustn't tell Walter about the party* and *You don't have to tell Walter about the party*. In the first one, the speaker is forbidding the listener from telling Walter about it: maybe the party is a surprise and he can't know about it. The second one would be appropriate if Walter already knows about the party: here the subject is saying that there is no longer an obligation to tell him, as in *Hey Bruno, you don't have to tell him about the party. I already did it and he said that he was coming*.

Denis: I imagine that in the first one, the speaker's tone of voice would have more force in it.

Geek: Yeah, it probably would. In addition to necessity, the modal *must* is also used to express logicality; in other words, a logical deduction, or inference. Suppose your Mom calls you up to inform you that her cousin Jeb, whom you have never seen before, is going to be passing through town the next day and will probably stop in at the lounge. She also mentions that he now lives in the United States and that he is a huge Donald Trump fan. The next day, you start your shift and a man wearing a red *Make America Great Again* hat struts into the lounge and sits down. You walk up to his table and say *Hello there. You must be my Mom's cousin Jeb!*

Denis: Ha! I think that I would also ask him to kindly remove his hat... heh heh.

Geek: That is an example of what I mean by logicality. In my example, you make a deduction based on the red hat, which represents evidence. We also make deductions in a different way with *must*. Suppose you are waiting for some friends to arrive from Calgary who said that they might stop at a rest stop to eat lunch. Looking at your watch and seeing that they still haven't arrived, you could deduce that *they must have stopped for lunch*.

Denis: Is that like saying *Ils ont dû arreter pour diner*?

Geek: Yes, it is. The last thing you need to know about *must* is that it doesn't have a past or future form. If you have a sentence in French like *J'ai dû revenir à la maison* or *Tu devras le rapporter demain* you translate these with a form of *have to*: *I had to come back home* and *You will have to bring it back tomorrow*.

Denis: Nice to know.

Geek: The final modal we will look at is *would*. It can express desire, as in *I would like a hot dog*, past habit, as in *When I was young, my mom would always read me a bedtime story*, and preference, as in *I would rather see a movie instead*. You also see it in conditional sentences. Those are sentences that express the relationship if X, then Y; that is, there is a condition and a consequence. For example, *If someone stole my cell phone, I would be upset*.

Denis: I see. But sometimes people say *will* too, right? As in "I will be upset".

Geek: Yes, they do. You are really getting to be a keen observer of English. There are, in fact, two kinds of conditional sentence. The first is what grammarians call the real condition, where the condition actually happens, or has high chances of happening. Examples are *If Susan drinks too much, she always regrets it* or *If Susan drinks too much, she will regret it*.

Lesson 6: Modals and Conditionals

Denis: Oh okay, I see. So what is the second kind?

Geek: The second type of conditional is the unreal condition. We use this type when the condition has little to no chance of happening. It has a much more hypothetical tone, as in *I know I never will, but if I won the lottery, I would buy a new Porsche*. We also use this type when the condition did not happen at all, as in *If I had won a million dollars, I would have bought a new Porsche*.

Denis: So let me get all those verbs straight. I can say *If I have time, I do it, If I have time, I will do it, If I had time, I would do it* and *If I had had time, I would have done it*?

Geek: All of those are perfectly acceptable. Well done!

Denis: Good. So I see that it is time for us to say our goodbyes for today. Once again, I need to get back to work. The manager just came in too and he is probably wondering why I am sitting here talking to a client and not serving the ones that just walked in!

Geek: Yes, he probably is... as we say in English, duty calls! Oops, and speaking of duty calling there goes my cell again. My kids want to know if I can meet them over at the pool so I have to scoot.

Denis: See you tomorrow!

Geek: See you tomorrow!

Exercises, lesson 6
Part 1: Editing
Correct the modal mistakes in the following sentences.

1. If you ask me, I think that people must eating at least one poutine per week.
2. He will comes to see us tomorrow, okay?
3. When I was young, I can eat 10 Big Macs in one sitting.
4. Yesterday, Julie must take the bus home.
5. When you can give me your homework?
6. People should to spend less time on social media.
7. Do you can speak German when you were little?
8. He gonna bring some chips for the party.

Part 2: Modals

Choose the best modal phrase. Make a sentence with the modal phrase that you did not choose.

1. I <u>may see her/can see her</u> at the party later. What does she look like?
2. I promise. I <u>will not lose my temper again/ must not lose my temper again</u>.
3. We thought that he <u>will be disappointed / would be disappointed</u>.
4. I <u>will be a bit more careful / would be a bit more careful</u> if I were you.
5. Because of the snowstorm, the train <u>can be an hour or two late / may be an hour or two late</u>.
6. Put a picnic in your backpack - the journey <u>might take hours / must take hours</u>.
7. She told me that the children <u>can be very noisy / should be very noisy</u> while getting ready for bed.
8. <u>Would you work harder/ Would you have worked harder</u> if you had been paid?
9. We have no inkling as to what the noise was - it <u>could have been the cat / must have been the cat</u>.
10. I <u>could get in touch with Steven / was able to get in touch with Steven</u> last night. He said that he is coming tomorrow.
11. Be careful when you travel in Africa. I was there last year and it <u>can be dangerous / may be dangerous</u>. Trust me.
12. I <u>could have said I was sorry/ must have said I was sorry</u>, but I didn't.
13. Mr. Foster <u>must be in his office/ can be in his office</u>. I see a light on.
14. You <u>must not talk to John about it / don't have to talk to John about it</u>. I already told him.
15. I don't see a sign anywhere. What do you think? <u>Can we park here / May we park here</u>?

Lesson 6: Modals and Conditionals

Part 3: Translation

Translate the following sentences. Use the correct modal for the underlined verbs[2].

1. Je <u>pouvais</u> prendre l'auto sans permission quand je restais chez mes parents.
2. Je <u>ne peux pas</u> vous le dire mais je <u>pourrais</u> le demander au patron.
3. <u>Il se peut qu'il fasse</u> froid demain. Tu <u>devrais</u> apporter un manteau.
4. J'<u>ai pu</u> changer mon horaire ce matin, alors je <u>pourrai</u> jouer au tennis avec toi demain.
5. Il <u>pourrait</u> avoir des meilleures notes s'il le voulait.
6. Nous <u>ne pouvons pas</u> le faire aujourd'hui mais nous <u>pourrons</u> le faire demain.
7. Je pense que je <u>vais pouvoir</u> vous aider.
8. Est-ce que tu <u>pourrais</u> me rencontrer demain?
9. Si tu me l'avais dit, j'<u>aurais pu</u> t'aider.
10. Il <u>a pu</u> convaincre ses parents de payer ses études.
11. Il <u>faut absolument</u> que tu lises ce livre.
12. Mon médecin m'a dit qu'il <u>ne faut pas</u> que j'oublie de prendre mes médicaments.
13. Il <u>doit bien avoir</u> une soixantaine d'années.
14. Tu <u>n'es pas obligé</u> d'apporter tes gants de boxe ce soir. Je <u>pourrai</u> te prêter les miens.
15. Il est furieux! Il <u>a dû</u> perdre aux échecs encore.
16. Tu <u>devras</u> apporter ton lunch à la rencontre.
17. Est-ce que je <u>devrais</u> consulter un médecin?
18. Si je gagne un million de dollars, je vous <u>amènerai</u> à Las Vegas.
19. Si je gagnais un million de dollars, je vous <u>achèterais</u> une maison aux Bahamas.
20. Si j'avais gagné un million de dollars, je vous <u>aurais donné</u> chacun dix milles dollars.

---

[2] A translation guide for certain modal phrases is included in the Reference Section.

Part 4: Contexts

Contextualize the following a pairs of sentences using at least 15 words each.

1. a) Jean-François could eat a dozen apples a day.

    b) Jean-François ate a dozen apples a day.

2. a) She is funny.

    b) She can be funny.

3. a) He can play the piano.

    b) He could play the piano.

4. a) College can be difficult.

    b) College may be difficult.

5. a) He can be a nice guy.

    b) He may be a nice guy.

6. a) They can come tonight.

    b) They may come tonight.

7. a) You shouldn't eat spicy food.

    b) You mustn't eat spicy food.

8. a) She had to leave early.

    b) She must have left early.

9. a) Would you buy one?

    b) Will you buy one?

10. a) Can we use these computers?

    b) May we use these computers?

11. a) You mustn't feed the canary.

    b) You don't have to feed the canary.

12. a) He was really grumpy.

    b) He could be really grumpy.

Part 5: Conditionals

Complete each of the following conditional sentences. When you are finished, practice by making conditional sentences of your own.

1. The teacher will help you…

2. What will you tell him…

3. If you spoke three languages…

4. If you do your homework…

5. If he plays sports…

6. If you had paid attention…

7. People would be happier…

8. If you had been there…

9. If social media did not exist…

10. If they arrive late…

11. If I were the prime minister…

12. No one would believe you…

13. We wouldn't have survived…

14. If I had more free time…

15. If she had had more money…

Lesson 7:
Nouns and pronouns

Denis: Bon après-midi Mr. Syme! Here you go... I've already poured you a pint.

Geek: A good afternoon to you too. Mmm. That's good stuff. So what's new with you?

Denis: Not too much... life is good! And this place is dead as usual. How about you? You look like you got some sun today.

Geek: Yes, I did indeed. The family and I spent the afternoon canoeing on the Bow River. The kids were in good spirits today... I packed extra snacks this time.

Denis: Good thinking. The Bow River is nice. So, changing subjects, what are we going to talk about today? I am having envy for some more grammar!

Geek: Careful there... you mean *I am eager for* some more grammar. Didn't your mother ever tell you about false friends?

Denis: Yeah right... the only words my mother knows in English are *yes no Toaster* and *Tupperware*. She can't even say Facebook. She says "Face de Book"!

Geek: Ouch! Okay then, she is forgiven. False friends are words that look the same or similar in two languages but have different meanings. *Envy* and *envie* do not mean the same thing. There are others too like *actually* and *actuellement*, *coin* and *coin*, or *library* and *librairie*. There are some that could put you in an embarrassing situation if you are not careful: *bra* and *bras*, *douche* and *douche*, or *preservative* and *préservatif*. Watch out there: if someone calls you a douche, he is not calling you a shower!

Denis: Well I knew that we could have false friends in life... now I see that there are false friends in grammar too! So is that going to be the subject of today's lesson?

Geek: Well, sort of. We have gotten off on a tangent but it does kind of lead into what I was planning on doing today. We have spent the past week discussing the verbal forms of English but today I thought that it is about time that we shifted gears and looked at some nominal forms.

Denis: That sounds great to me, Mr. Expert. So what do you mean by nominal form?

Geek: Well that's just another fancy term that us grammarians like to use to make ourselves sound smart. I am sure you have heard the terms 'noun' and 'pronoun' before?

Denis: Oh! *Le nom et le pronom*. Yes, of course I have. Back in school. My teacher said that nouns were a person, place, or thing. Pronouns can be used to substitute for them, right?

Geek: Very good. So let's start by reviewing the basics. First there are the basic pronouns *I, you, he, she, it, we,* and *they*. These are what we call subject pronouns because they are used as the subject of a sentence. Next there are *me, you, him, her, it, us* and *them*. These are what we call object pronouns because they are used as the object of a verb, as in 'Give *me* the bill' or 'I showed *them* the menu'.

Denis: Got it.

Geek: Next there are the pronouns *mine, yours, his, hers, ours* and *theirs*. These are what we call the possessive pronouns. Related to the possessive pronouns are the possessive adjectives *my, your, his, her, its, our* and *their*. The difference between the two is not always clear for ESL students and they can mix them up. We say *This is his book* or *This is his*. Likewise we say *This is her book* or *This is hers*. One big no-no is to do something like *Those are theirs books* or *These are ours pens*. In French your adjective agrees with the noun but not in English. No s-ending.

Denis: Right. I'll watch out for that.

Geek: The last set of pronouns I'll mention are *myself, yourself, himself, herself, itself, ourselves, yourselves* and *themselves*. These are used to refer back to the subject, who is both the one doing and receiving the action. A sentence like *Tim is serving himself* is different from *Tim is serving him*. In both cases Tim is doing the serving but the recipients of this action are, respectively, Tim and someone else. Another thing to watch out for is the difference between *yourself* and *yourselves*. If I say *Do it yourself*, I am addressing myself to one person. If I am addressing more than one person, I would have to say *Do it yourselves*.

Denis: O.k., that's clear now.

Geek: Before we go on to look at nouns, there are a few things that I'll mention in particular with regards to the pronouns that are common mistakes for Francophones. The first thing to remember is that in French, the pronoun that a person uses is determined by the gender of the noun it precedes. Since *chien* is masculine you say *son chien* and since *voiture* is feminine you say *sa voiture*. In English, the pronoun is determined by the gender of the subject, not the noun, so we say *his dog* or *her dog* depending on whether the subject is male or female. You have to be careful with objects too: if you are referring to the windows of a building, a building is an inanimate object so you need to say *its* windows and not his or her.

Denis: O.k. What about an animal? Do I use he, she or it?

Geek: Typically we only use he or she if we want to signal that there is a personal relationship to the animal. This is why a person will say, in reference to their pet cat, *She is outside* or *He's scratching at the door again*. It is very common in scientific writing where the author has no personal attachment to the animal in question: *The mountain gorilla is one of the two subspecies of the eastern gorilla. It is listed as an endangered species.*

Denis: I see... Grammar Gorilla.

Geek: Another thing that you want to avoid is combining a pronoun with a noun, something that you do all the time in spoken French as in *Ma mère, elle aime le spaghetti* or *Moi, je pense que tu as raison*. In English we simply say *My mom likes spaghetti* or *I think that you are right*.

Denis: I think I have heard people saying "Personally I think that you are right". Is that o.k.?

Geek: Yes, that is o.k. too. Another common mistake is something like *Everyone brought his dog to the park*. You don't want to be accused of being sexist by assuming that everyone is male so you need to say *Everyone brought his or her dog* or the more colloquial *their* dog.

Denis: Darn, I think I say that mistake a lot.

Geek: Well that's about it for the pronouns. Let's talk about nouns now.

Denis: Yes! Let's!

Geek: One distinction that is made is that of singular versus plural. To make most nouns plural, you are no doubt familiar with the fact that in English we add an 's'. For nouns ending in –s, -sh, -ch, -z, or –x, however, you need to add an *es*, like in *glasses, dishes, watches, buzzes,* or *boxes* and for nouns ending in –y you need to drop it and add *ies* as in *lotteries* or *studies*.

Denis: Yeah, that's easy.

Geek: In addition to these 'regular' plurals, there are nouns which don't follow the standard rule. These are the irregular plurals. There are cases where the central vowel is changed, as in tooth/teeth, foot/feet, man/men, woman/women, goose/geese, mouse/mice, etc. There are cases where you add –en: child/children and ox/oxen. There are cases where the –f becomes a –v as in leaf/leaves or shelf/shelves. In addition to these are words that come from Latin, such as stimulus/stimuli, bacterium/bacteria, phenomenon/phenomena as well as words ending in –is: analysis/analyses, crisis/crises. There are also nouns which don't change at all: deer/deer, sheep/sheep, fish/fish, series/series, offspring/offspring, etc.

Denis: Wow. That is quite the list!

Geek: In terms of singular and plural nouns, there are other things that you need to watch out for. There are some nouns which are always plural: pants, clothes, binoculars, savings, pajamas, and shorts. For these nouns, the verb is also plural: *My pants are too tight* or *My savings are dwindling*. There are other nouns which are always plural but do not take a plural verb like mathematics, economics, politics, news, and physics. You need to say *Mathematics is fun* or *Fake news is bad for you*.

In addition to the singular-plural distinction, there is also the count/non-count distinction. In English, like in French, some nouns can be counted: I have two cars, three cats, ten plates, six thing-a-ma-jigs, et cetera. Where the difficulty lies is in the nouns which are count in French but non-count in English. In French you can say *un devoir* or *des devoirs* but in English you can't say *a* homework or *some homeworks*.

Denis: Oops. I think I said homeworks when I was in school. I notice too that sometimes my French friends say 'a bread' but that sounds wrong to me.

Geek: Yes, in some cases you need to add a quantifier in order to specify that you are referring to a unit. For bread, you use *loaf* and so you say *a loaf of bread*. The same goes for toast; you need to say a piece of toast, a slice of toast, or two pieces, slices, and so on.

Denis: So that takes care of breakfast. What other nouns should I watch out for?

Geek: Watch out for *information*, *advice* and *evidence*. You can't say an information, an advice, or an evidence: you need to add the word *piece*. Hence you say a *piece* of information, a *piece* of advice or a *piece* of evidence.

Denis: Ha! And I thought you could only say a *piece* of cake or a *piece* of pizza.

Geek: There are also other words you can use to talk about units too: a *bar* of soap, a *pair* of pants, a *cup* of coffee, and so on. Always check a dictionary if you aren't sure. You carry around a cellphone with WiFi wherever you go, don't you?

Denis: Indeed I do!

Geek: Sometimes in order to refer to a unit of something, instead of adding a unitizing word like piece, you need to add another word after the noun. Hence *un logiciel* is not *a software* but a software *program*. In other cases, you can actually refer to the nature of the item itself. So while you can say *a piece of luggage*, you could also say *suitcase* or *bag*. Instead of a *piece of furniture*, say whether it's a *couch*, a *chair*, or a *desk*. Instead of homework, say an *assignment* or instead of research say a *study*.

Denis: Good to know. I have a question about the word *garbage* and *hair* though. In French we say *les déchets* but there is no 's' on garbage in English, right?

Geek: Right. So we say the garbage *is* being picked up.

Denis: And you always say something like "Her hair is dyed blue" and never "Her hairs are dyed blue", right?

Geek: Yes. The only time hair can be pluralized is in something like *The police found some brown hairs at the crime scene*.

Denis: Alright. Got it.

Geek: So before we wrap up our discussion on nouns I'll say a little something about the genitive form, or apostrophe 's'. This form is used to describe a relationship between two nouns. The most common way of using the genitive is to express possession, as in *My Dad's boat* or *My parents' house*. We can get fancier too and say *My Dad's brother's boat*. It is also not ungrammatical to say *My mom's sister's husband's son's new car*.

Denis: Yikes. That is a bit confusing though.

Geek: Indeed it is, which is why we would probably find a way around saying it like "My mom has a sister and that is her husband's son's new car".

Denis: Or I guess you could just say "My cousin's new car", right?

Geek: Eek! You are correct. Now the genitive does not always express a relationship of possession. In some cases, the genitive noun is the doer of the main noun: *the customer's complaint* or *the manager's proposal*. In others, the genitive noun is the object of the main noun: *the prisoner's release* the *child's punishment*. It can also express the kind of thing one is referring to. If I say *the men's room* or *a boys' school* then I mean 'the room for men' or 'a school for boys'. Finally, it can be used to express time. Incidentally, how much sleep did you get last night?

Denis: I think I slept for about four hours.

Geek: In other words, you could say that you got *four hours' sleep*.

Denis: Nice expression. So next week, I am going to finally have two days off… could I say that I will have *two days' vacation*?

Geek: You catch on fast. Yes, you could. In fact, one way to really improve your English, and what I tell my students, is to use the genitive more often. In French you use the preposition 'de' to indicate a genitive relationship, which is why French speakers have a tendency to overuse the 'of' phrase in English. Instead of saying *the company of my father* say *My father's company*. Instead of *the guests of the hotel* say *the hotel's guests*. And so on and so forth.

Denis: Is there a way to know when to use the genitive and not the *of* phrase?

Geek: One tip I can give you is that genitive is preferred with nouns referring to human beings or domesticated animals: instead of saying *the hat of Bob* or *the litter box of my cat*, say *Bob's hat* or *the cat's litter box*. It is also preferred with institutions so don't say the *budget of the government* or *the students of the university*.

Denis: I need to say *the government's budget* or *the university's students*. Great. I think I've got it.

Geek: Finally, in addition to the uses we have been looking at, there is something called the independent genitive in which there is no noun following the apostrophes. Instead of saying *That is Antoine's toy* or *Tom's car is on the right* it is possible to say a sentence like *That toy is Antoine's* or *Tom's is the car on the right*. Common uses of the independent genitive involve homes, churches, doctors, or dentists: I'm staying at my *parents'*, We attend St. *Vincent's*, or I'm going to the *dentist's*. It can even be combined with the *of* phrase to get He is a friend of my *mom's*.

Denis: Neat. I don't think I ever say those things so I feel like my English just got a lot better. I think I will make it my mission to try to use the genitive tonight with my customers.

Geek: Perfect. I must say that it's nice to have such an eager student.

Denis: I told you when we first met that I would be a good student. So are you going to hang out here in the lounge or head back up to your room? I imagine that your family is waiting again?

Geek: Nope, they've gone out for some souvenir shopping and will not be back for a while. That means I can stay for another pint.

Denis: Well then, here you go. A pint for the Geek. Hey, it's the Geek's pint!

Geek: Santé!

Exercises, lesson 7

Part 1: Pronoun review

Fill in the blank with the correct pronoun. The referents are in italics.

1. *Cindy* called. Please call _____ back at 2 pm. _____ says that it is urgent.

2. *Jane and I* are going shopping. Do you want to come with _____?

3. *The parcel* is at the post office. Please collect _____ this afternoon.

4. *The city of Victoria* is known for _____ beautiful gardens.

5. Those books on the table belong to *Amanda*. They are _____.

6. *Julie* is sick today. Give _____ two aspirins at lunchtime.

7. *We* gave them _____ telephone number and *they* gave us _____.

8. You can't have any of *my* chocolate. It is all _____!

9. *Tara and Marie* own a bakery and I work with _____ a lot.

10. When nobody is at home, *Horace and Daisy* can work by _____.

11. If you go to a job interview, *you* should wear _____ best clothes.

12. When *Alice* called, *I* talked to _____. She asked _____ for the English homework.

Lesson 7: Nouns and pronouns

13. *Sam* has a dinner invitation. *Mr. and Mrs. Smith* want _____ to come to _____ house. *He* is taking _____ new car to go there.

14. *Geoff and Steven* are talking to *Chris and Lynn* over there. I wonder what language _____ are speaking to _____.

15. *My grandmother* is very old; _____ is celebrating _____ 87th birthday this week!

16. Sometimes, *Alex* works by _____ and we work by _____.

17. *I* lost my textbooks. If you find *my books*, please return _____ to _____.

18. My friend and _____ have a lot in common. *We* both love to play soccer and video games.

19. *Emile* collects old hockey cards. This Sidney Crosby rookie card belongs to him. It is _____.

20. *All students* need to hand in _____ assignments by November 1.

The following paragraph has 10 pronoun mistakes. Identify the mistake and make the correction.

My Uncle Keith influenced me a lot in my life because his so talented. Keith his a passionate singer for the Rolling Stones. Is guitars are extremely expensive. He likes to record music with his group or by hisself. Sometimes, i visit my uncle's studio. If your looking for some good music, you should buy one of his albums. Its not hard to find them second hand. Do you need a singer for you're wedding? Maybe the Rolling Stones they could play for you! Their always excited to play for anyone.

Part 2: Count and non-count nouns

Fill in the information below. Use a dictionary to help you find the correct way to quantify each noun.

Noun	French	English
advice	un conseil	a piece of/some advice
research	une recherche	a study/some research
information		
software		
homework		
furniture		
luggage		
lightning		
evidence		
soap		
bread		
toast		
garbage		
jewelry		
equipment		

Part 3: Translation

Translate the following.

1. J'ai acheté un pain hier alors nous pouvons tous prendre trois toasts avec nos céréales ce matin.
2. Jean a un petit conseil à te donner pour ton voyage au Mexique : identifie bien tes bagages avant de partir.
3. Cela me dérange quand les animaux se couchent sur les meubles.
4. J'ai une bonne nouvelle: vous allez pouvoir continuer vos recherches même si vous n'avez pas obtenu la subvention.
5. Je n'ai pas fait mes devoirs en philo parce qu'il me manque des informations.
6. La semaine passée, les déchets n'ont pas été ramassés.
7. Tiens! Un autre éclair! Va chercher les jumelles tout de suite. Elles sont sur la table.
8. L'hiver je prends quatre rôties avec de la confiture et un café le matin.
9. Nous ne pouvons pas procéder avec le procès si vous n'avez pas de preuves.

Part 4: Editing

Correct the plural mistakes in the following sentences.

1. There are not evidences to support the detectives' various hypothesis.
2. There is only one criteria for the job: you must speak at least two language.
3. My chiropractor offered me some very practicals advices.
4. A lack of motivation is one of the main reason that college student drop out.
5. She loves politic so when she finishes her study she wants to explore others countries.

6. All of the analysis have come back and the result are all negatives.

7. According to expert, the country is undergoing several food crisis at the moment.

8. I like to buy tights clothes but this pants is way too tight.

9. Mathematics are my favourite subject but I also like Physic.

10. Do you have any informations about our lost luggages?

Part 5: The genitive

Change the underlined words to the genitive.

1. It was in <u>the paper of yesterday</u>.

2. Van Houten is reputed to produce <u>the best chocolate in the world</u>.

3. <u>The car of my neighbor</u> got stolen last night.

4. I don't like <u>songs of the Beatles</u>.

5. They have lobster on <u>the menu of today</u>.

6. Rivière-du-loup is <u>a drive of two hours from Quebec</u>.

7. <u>The parents of all the other boys</u> were present.

8. Every day I have to pick up <u>the toys of my children</u>.

9. This pen belongs to Tom. It is...

10. <u>The orders of the commander-in-chief</u> have to be obeyed.

11. <u>The Mustang of my father-in-law</u> is off-limits.

12. <u>The sister of the friend of Daniel</u> lives beside us.

13. I do not agree with <u>the policies of this government</u> at all.

14. Everyone will stop after <u>a workout of twenty minutes</u>.

15. They are investigating <u>the murder of Mr. White</u>.

Lesson 8: Adverbs and Adjectives

Denis: Well look who's here everyone... the one... the only... Grammar Geek!

Geek: Good afternoon Denis. How are things?

Denis: Great thanks. So what adventures did you have with the family today?

Geek: Well, we did some hiking and I had the good fortune of being able to teach my kids a valuable lesson in the process.

Denis: Oh yeah? What was it? Please share.

Geek: Well we were hiking along the trail and about 10 minutes into our hike, my kids started whining again. Sore feet, thirst, hunger,... all the usual stuff. As if by providence, I spotted deer turds on the trail and had a great idea. Scooping them up in my hand, I showed them to my kids and asked them if they knew what they were. As I had anticipated, they had no idea and so I told them what they were. I informed them that they were... get this... smart pills.

Denis: Smart pills? I've heard of smart phones and smart televisions but not smart *pills*.

Geek: Oh no? Well here is what happened. I told them that if they ate one of them, they would become smarter. Believing that the more they ate the smarter they would become, each of them scooped a few up and popped them in their mouths. My daughter was the first to realize that something wasn't right and wincing in disgust, she looked up at me and said "Ugh, Dad, that tasted like crap". I replied, "And I bet you won't ever eat them again. See? You're getting smarter already."

Denis: Ugh! No way! Isn't that like... child abuse...?!

Geek: You should have seen the look on their faces! They were so mad at me that they didn't say another word to me until we got back here to the hotel.

Denis: And will they ever talk to you again?

Geek: Oh heck yeah. I smoothed things over before I came here with an offer of ice cream and a movie. They have forgiven me. My wife though… I don't think she will be nominating me for father of the year anytime soon.

Denis: Well now I know what to do if you offer me anything "smart" in the future. Run away!

Geek: Now you are scared, eh? So now that I have gotten that little anecdote off of my chest, are you ready to get down to some grammar?

Denis: I am. So what are we going to talk about today?

Geek: Let's get on with it then. So far we have covered a lot of ground in terms of nouns and verbs so I was thinking that it would be a good time to talk about the words we use to describe them: adjectives and adverbs.

Denis: Sounds great.

Geek: Adjectives and adverbs are used to describe other words. If I say *a smart teacher* then the adjective *smart* tells us about the noun *teacher*. I could then add an adverb and say *an extremely smart teacher*. In this case, the adverb *extremely* tells us how *smart* applies to teacher: it says that the teacher's smartness is to a high degree.

Denis: That makes sense so far.

Geek: Let's begin with how they are used in comparing and contrasting things. There are three ways which we can use to compare and contrast. The first way is *equative*: this is where two nouns are said to possess the quality expressed by the adjective or adverb to equal degrees. An example of this would be *Boys are as smart as girls* or *This laptop runs as efficiently as that one*. The second way is *comparative*, which is where one noun is said to possess the quality expressed by the adjective or adverb in a greater or lesser degree than the other. For example: *Girls are smarter than boys* or *A turtle moves less quickly than a hare*. Finally, the third way is the superlative: here one noun

Lesson 8: Adverbs and Adjectives

is said to possess the quality in question to a higher degree than all members of the group of which it is part. For example, *Andrew is the smartest man in the world* or *Shakespeare was the most brilliant playwright of his time.*

Denis: Equative, comparative, superlative. Three ways. Got it. But I think sometimes you use an –er ending and sometimes you use the word *more* or *less* when you are comparing and contrasting nouns, don't you? I'm thinking of a sentence like *My book is more interesting than your book.* What's going on there?

Geek: Yes, we don't say *interestinger* or the *interestingest*. Luckily, there are some ways to decide whether you should use the –er and –est or not. First of all, you can ask yourself if the adjective or adverb has one syllable. If it does, then you use the –er. Thus *big* and *small* are *bigger* and *smaller*. *Old* and *young* are *older* and *younger*. You don't say *more old* and *more young*, which is what you do in French: *plus vieux* or *plus jeune*.

Denis: Darn French again… Always interfering with what we want to say!

Geek: Now then, with adjectives or adverbs with two or more syllables, you need to use *more* and *most*. The word *interesting* has three syllables which is why we use these words. With an adjective like *acceptable* we say *more/less acceptable* or *the most/least acceptable*. The exceptions to this pattern are adjectives like *tasty, simple,* and *yellow*: these all end in *y*, *le*, and *ow* and are treated the same way as one-syllable adjectives. Hence you need to say tastier/the tastiest, simpler/the simplest and yellower/the yellowest. Adverbs do not have this exception however. Even if they end in y, you still stick to the more/most and less/least rule: *Phelps swam more rapidly than the others* or *Phelps swam the most rapidly.*

Denis: O.k., so let me make sure that I understand. If I am talking about a bowl of pretzels and comparing their salty taste, I could say *These pretzels are saltier than those ones* or *They are the healthiest kind that you can buy*. I think that I say things like *more tasty* or *more healthy* sometimes. Oops.

Geek: Yeah, I know. Some foreign language speakers also say *more tastier* or *more healthier*, which are also big no-nos. Another common mistake for Francophones is to translate a sentence like *Le coke est* *plus goûteux que le pepsi* as *Coke is tastier that Pepsi*. You need to watch out for that one too: *que* often translates as *that*, but not in comparatives.

Denis: Got it. There's French interference again.

Geek: Another thing to note about comparisons is irregular adjective forms. The comparative forms of *good* and *bad* are *as good as*, *better*, and *the best* and *as bad as*, *worse* and *the worst*. There are other interesting things we can discuss about adjectives and adverbs which you need to be careful about too. One thing relates to their position in a sentence. For adjectives, it is pretty straightforward: the adjective precedes the noun it applies to, as we saw with *smart pill*: we don't say *pill smart*. For adverbs, the picture isn't quite that simple though because they are more mobile. In some cases, it doesn't matter where you put the adverb in terms of meaning. If I say *By then, they were in Regina* or *They were in Regina by then*, then you get the same message. However, there are cases where the position of the adverb makes a difference.

Denis: Oh yeah?

Geek: Take the adverb *honestly* for instance. I could say *Honestly, I didn't do my homework* or *I didn't do my homework honestly*. In which one did the person actually do their homework?

Denis: Hmm. The second one, right?

Geek: Exactly. In the first one, the subject is saying "I am being honest about the fact that I didn't do my homework". In the second one the subject is coming clean: he is saying that he did his homework, but not in an honest manner. Maybe he copied off of someone or got his older brother to do it.

Denis: Gee, I never did that! What other ones can you tell me about?

Geek: Take the word *generously*. There is a difference between *Microsoft generously donated to the cause* and *Microsoft donated to the cause generously*. In the first sentence generously tells us more about the subject, in this case the company: It was generous of the company to donate. They could have chosen not to donate at all but they didn't. In the second sentence, generously tells us more about the manner in which it donated. Here we get a clearer indication as to the amount of money that they gave: they gave a generous amount.

Lesson 8: Adverbs and Adjectives

Denis: Yeah. I get it. Maybe in the first one they only gave a few pennies.

Geek: Right. Other adverbs that behave this way are *politely*, *rudely* and *kindly*. A third difference you get in terms of adverb position is with a case like *He clearly can't hear us* and *He can't hear us clearly*. In one of these cases the subject can actually hear, albeit just a little bit.

Denis: The second one.

Geek: Right you are. In the first one, it is like saying '*It is clear that he can't hear*', as in *It's safe now, don't worry. You can tell me what you got Joey for his birthday. He clearly can't hear us as he's got his headphones on with the music up.* In the second one, the message is that the subject can hear, but not clearly as in *Grandpa can't hear us clearly. He can understand a few words but he has problems understanding everything. He should get his ears examined.*

Denis: O.k. So are there other things that I should know about adverbs and adjectives?

Geek: Yes. One thing that can be confusing for English learners is what order to place them in when you have more than one. Let's look at adverbs and what we call adverbial phrases first, as it is a bit more straightforward. Sometimes, length is a determining factor. You need to put the longer one at the end: *He ate the burger quickly in a sloppy way.* In other cases, where the adverbials are of the same length, meaning is the determining factor. You need to think in terms of MPT: manner, place and time. If I say *They hiked* and the adverbs *up the mountain*, *slowly*, and *yesterday* then you need to follow the order of manner first, then place, and then time: *They hiked slowly up the mountain yesterday.*

Denis: Got it. But what if I have two places? Do I say *He got his degree at the University of Calgary in Alberta*, or *He got his degree in Alberta at the University of Calgary*? And what if there is more than one time expression?

Geek: For places, we typically go from the smaller area to the bigger one, so the first one would be the better choice: *at the University of Calgary in Alberta*. With time adverb expressions, they tend to occur in the order DFW: duration, frequency and when. If you have *at noon*, *every day* and *for 10 minutes* then you need to say *They met for 10 minutes every day at noon*. If you have two whens, either order is possible: *We met at noon yesterday* is the same as *We met yesterday at noon*.

Denis: Great.

Geek: Finally we come to adjectives. There is, believe it or not, an order to the adjectives in a sentence like *A big, beautiful, round, chipped, ancient, blue, Italian vase*. The formula that you need to remember is... get ready for this one... A-S-O-S-C-A-C-O-M. It is pronounced *azz-o-skack-om*. Say it.

Denis: Azz-o-skack-om?

Geek: Ha ha! I know, it sounds pretty bad, but it's the best that I could come up with, honestly. Let me walk you through them: A is for *article*, as in *the, a,* or *an*, or any other determiner for that matter: many, several, some, etc. S is for *size*, like *small, huge, giant*, and so on. O is for *opinion*: *ugly, beautiful, nice, difficult,* etc. The second S is for *shape*: *flat, square, rectangular*, etc. C is for *condition*, A is for *age*, the next C is for *color*, and the O is for *origin*: Gothic, German, Scottish, etc. The M is for *material*: wood, cotton, oak, etc.

Denis: Wow. That's a lot to process. Can we try some exercises to check my understanding?

Geek: How about this: you are thinking about a girl that you met at the bar last night who was attractive, from the United States, and single.

Denis: Let's see. So attractive is an opinion, single is a condition, and her origin is American so I would say an attractive, single, American girl.

Geek: Right. Let's suppose that you are craving some beer from Ireland that is ice-cold and that you are heading to a pub that is Irish, quaint, and old-fashioned.

Denis: Ha ha. I would say I am going to a quaint (opinion), old-fashioned (age) Irish pub (origin) to have some ice-cold (condition) Irish (origin) beer.

Geek: Very good. Like I have said before, you catch on quite fast. So that about wraps up things for today.

Lesson 8: Adverbs and Adjectives

Denis: Great. I need to get back to serving my customers. More specifically, *my friendly English customers* with *their strange square English heads.*

Geek: Ooh, ouch! Stop it… that hurts. You stop that right now or I will have to bring out the demeaning French jokes. You know, the ones which involve a certain green amphibian?

Denis: Ah! O.k., o.k., you win. So will I be seeing you tomorrow?

Geek: Of course you will. *Adieu!*

Exercises, lesson 8
Part 1: Comparisons with adjectives
Complete the comparison with the adjective in parentheses.

Examples:

Rose is (intelligent) as the other students.
Answer: *as intelligent*

This movie is (interesting) than that one.
Answer: *more/less interesting*

Yogi is (calm) dog in the litter.
Answer: *the calmest*

1. Mr. Ross is (friendly) neighbor that I know.
2. John looks (nervous) than Jack.
3. Bill Gates is (rich) man in the world.
4. The manager is (popular) than the CEO.
5. My cat looks (old) than my dog.
6. Brady is (geeky) of all the players.
7. The weather is (cold) than usual today.
8. Ottawa is (far) from here than Montreal.
9. His test mark was (bad) than mine.
10. The earthquake is (bad) in modern history.
11. Those guys are (cheerful) than those girls.
12. He is (bratty) than the other children.
13. Antoine is (sensitive) as all the children.

14. Hubert's drawing was (good) than Frank's.
15. Greg's drawing was (good) out of the whole class.
16. We were feeling (happy) than them.
17. He was definitely (smart) man in the room.
18. Charlotte is (quiet) than Jason.

Part 2: Comparisons with adverbs

Complete the comparison with the adverb in parentheses.

1. Jeff speaks Japanese (fluently) than I.
2. Kyla plays the violin (skillfully) of all the students.
3. She attends class (often) as I do.
4. That speaker presented (calmly) than the other.
5. Jackie understands (well) than the rest of us.
6. We searched his house (thoroughly) than hers.
7. You will probably graduate (soon) than I.
8. She drives (badly) than her daughter.
9. I usually get up (early) than my brother.
10. That student worked (hard) than the others.
11. She treats people (well) of all the doctors.
12. My mom speaks (seriously) as my dad.
13. She sleeps (soundly) than her brother.
14. Doug will deliver it (quickly) than Keith.
15. Holly trains (regularly) of all the runners.
16. The mayor reacted (reasonably) than the premier.
17. Fred will run (fast) than anybody else.
18. Please apologize (sincerely) than that.
19. Ms. Lincoln worked (confidently) as Mr. Tangredi.
20. He sold (effectively) than other salespeople.

Lesson 8: Adverbs and Adjectives

Part 3: Contexts

Circle the correct answer.

1. In which of the following does the speaker know that Maryse spoke to Nancy?
    a) Hopefully Maryse spoke to Nancy about it.
    b) Maryse spoke to Nancy about it hopefully.

2. In which one is it possible that the CEO's donation was not a generous amount?
    a) The CEO generously donated to the cause.
    b) The CEO donated generously to the cause.

3. In which one is the speaker saying "I am being honest"?
    a) Honestly, we talked about it.
    b) We talked about it honestly.

4. In which one does the subject like his philosophy class just a little bit?
    a) He really doesn't like his philosophy class.
    b) He doesn't really like his philosophy class.

5. In which one is the speaker talking about his performance on the final exams?
    a) I found them easy.
    b) I found them easily.

6. In which one did the subject talk about it in a complex manner?
    a) He simply didn't talk about it.
    b) He didn't talk about it simply.

7. In which one did the man hear them?
    a) The man clearly didn't hear them.
    b) The man didn't hear them clearly.

8. In which one was the speaker's explanation done in a frank manner?
    a) Frankly, I explained the problem.
    b) I explained the problem frankly.
9. In which one does the speaker mean "It was polite of him to do that"?
    a) Vincent politely left the room.
    b) Vincent left the room politely.
10. In which one should the speaker warn David about the danger that he is in?
    a) That spider on David's back is dead.
    b) That spider on David's back is deadly.

Part 4: Word order

Rewrite each sentence with the adverbs in the correct order.

1. Take this. (to your mother, immediately)
2. I have been working. (all day, in this room)
3. He was born. (in 1943, in Paris)
4. They came up. (to the fire, a few minutes later)
5. I have been living. (at home, quietly, since 1950)
6. She spoke to him. (sternly, in the hall, after dinner)
7. I will meet you. (this evening, at the party)
8. I said good-bye to them. (regretfully, yesterday, at the station)
9. He has been sitting. (for 10 minutes, peacefully, on that chair)
10. Let's invite them. (to the theatre, tonight)
11. They are going. (for the weekend, to their cottage)
12. The plane arrived. (on time, at the airport)
13. He stopped. (very suddenly, at the stop sign, this morning)
14. I do exercise. (two times a week, for one hour, at the gym)
15. They talked. (in the restaurant, last year, every night, for two hours)

Lesson 8: Adverbs and Adjectives

Arrange the adjectives supplied in the correct order.

1. A cabin (big, log, brand-new)
2. Beer (Mexican, cold, some)
3. A girl (American, poor, teenaged)
4. A Camaro (gorgeous, antique)
5. An armchair (new, luxurious, IKEA)
6. A lecture (university, interesting)
7. Clothes (old, useless)
8. A head (large, square, English)
9. A vest (cute, brown)
10. A book (engaging, Spanish)
11. A garden (French, beautiful)
12. Food (delicious, Cantonese)
13. A man (annoying, elderly)
14. A hat (broad-rimmed, Mexican)
15. Table (fine, oak, old)

Lesson 9: Determiners – Part 1

Geek: Hello Denis! Hey, what's with all the decorations in here today? I see Quebec flags everywhere.

Denis: Hello Mr. Syme! Did you forget? Today is St-Jean Baptiste!

Geek: Well well… you are right. Goodness gracious, it is funny how disconnected we become when we are on vacation. *Bonne St-Jean mon ami*!

Denis: Same to you. So did you see our specials board today?

Geek: Yes, I glanced at it as I walked in. What does 'P P combo' mean?

Denis: Well that is the best name that I could think of. Today's promotion is in honour of St. Jean-Baptiste and my home province: P plus P equals poutine and a pint!

Geek: Ha! I should have guessed. I will definitely go for that. Extra gravy on the poutine *s'il vous plaît*.

Denis: No problem. And here is your pint… in the spirit of Quebec culture, a chilled *la fin du monde*.

Geek: Awesome. You Quebeckers sure know how to make beer. And hey, do you know what? It just so happens that I have got a great St. Jean Baptiste joke to put us in the mood for today.

Denis: Please please! I am always ready for one of your jokes.

Geek: Well here it is. So there was a man who thought he was John the Baptist and he was disturbing the neighborhood so for public safety, he was committed to a mental hospital. He was put in a room with another crazy and immediately began his routine, "I am John the Baptist! Jesus Christ has sent me!" The other guy looked at him and declared, "No I didn't!".

Denis: Ha! Once again, you have put a smile on my face and put me in the mood for some grammar.

Geek: Well actually, I see that there's no one around so why don't you pour yourself a little something and get comfortable? Today we are going to talk about... get ready for this... determiners!

Denis: That is an invitation that I cannot refuse. So tell me, please, what is a determiner in English?

Geek: Good, here we go. A determiner is a word or a group of words that comes before a noun and which is used to tell us about that noun. One type of determiner is the article. There are two articles in English: the definite article, *the*, and the indefinite article *a*, or *an* if the noun it precedes begins with a vowel sound. To this I would add a third one: the zero article, which basically is when there is no article. Articles can be confusing for French speakers learning English because of the differences between the two languages. A sentence such as *J'adore l'école* can be translated in two ways: either *I love the school* or *I love school*. Similarly, if your Mom were to call out *Le souper est prêt* then this would be translated only as *Supper is ready* and not *the* supper is ready.

Denis: Oh yeah. I never really noticed that before.

Geek: What I find really fascinating is that other languages don't have a distinct word for their articles. In Persian, *sib* is the word for *apple*. If I want to say *the apple* then I say *sibe*. In Icelandic the word for beer is *bjór* and *the* beer is *bjórinn*. Neat, eh?

Denis: Yeah. It sure is. So what can you tell me about the articles?

Geek: Let's start with the indefinite versus the definite article. What you need to keep in mind is that the indefinite article is used to indicate that you are referring to one thing out of a set of things. If I say *Would you like a French fry?* then I am offering you a plateful of them: I am offering you one out of the set of fries on my plate. The definite article points you to a specific fry. If I say *Would you like the French fry?* then I am offering you a plate with only one on it. Or I am offering you a choice between the French fry and the celery stick. Pretty generous of me, eh?

Denis: I'll take the fry please!

Lesson 9: Determiners – Part 1

Geek: O.k. then. In my experience, the difference between the indefinite and definite article is not too hard to grasp. The challenge is in learning the difference between the definite and the zero article. Can you explain to me the difference between a sentence like *I like people* or *I like the people*?

Denis: I'll give it a shot. In the first one, I think the subject is talking about all people, people in general. In the second one, the subject is being more specific. Maybe they are referring to the people at a specific place.

Geek: You are right. Maybe they mean this lounge: *I come to this lounge every night because the people here are so nice*. A similar example is *music* versus *the music*. If I say *Stephanie likes music* then I mean music in general; all music. If I say *Stephanie likes the music* then I am being more specific, as in *Usually Stephanie doesn't dance but look at her dance right now. She really likes the music that is playing at the moment*.

Denis: I see. So what else should I watch out for?

Geek: Another thing to watch out for is concepts or ideas like *freedom*, *truth*, *justice*, *beauty*, and *art*. In French you say *Au Québec nous valorisons la diversité* but in English we say *In Quebec we value diversity*. No article. Some popular examples include *Beauty is in the eye of the beholder* or *Fight for truth, justice and the American way*.

Denis: Got it.

Geek: So let's return to a sentence like 'J'adore l'école' which I mentioned can be translated in two ways: *I love school* or *I love the school*. Would you care to give those a try?

Denis: In the first one I get the impression that the person really enjoys going to school and learning. In the second, I get the impression he is referring to a specific school.

Geek: Precisely, as in *We are so happy that we left the city and moved out to this suburb. The people are friendly and I love the school*. In the first one, your context is perfect. When you want to refer to the activity associated with the noun, in this case learning and getting an education, then no article is used.

Denis: Neat. Are there other nouns like that?

Geek: Yes; *prison, church, tv,* and *bed* are some common ones. If I say *Uncle Wayne is in prison* then I mean that he is incarcerated. If I say *Julio is in church* then it is Sunday and he is there attending mass. If I say *I saw it on tv* then I could be referring to a product that I saw being advertised. Finally, if I say *I sent him to bed* then it means that I sent him to go to sleep.

Denis: I see... so incarceration, attending mass, advertising and sleeping are all activities associated with those nouns.

Geek: Indeed. Bed can be associated with sleep but also with other activities as well. If I were to say *I found Rob and Tina in bed* and Tina was my girlfriend, then what could you conclude about my relationship with Tina right now?

Denis: Ha. Over?

Geek: Yes indeed... sayonara, girl. Don't let the door hit you on the way out! So what about with the article now? When we use the article it is to refer to the actual building or object that the noun denotes. Suppose you are visiting an antique museum with your Uncle Wayne and he steps inside a prison display that has been set up for visitors. There you could say *Uncle Wayne is in the prison.* If you are referring to a crafts sale held by your local church then you would say *The event took place in the church.* Likewise, if you spot your cousin Todd dancing on top of the television then you could say *Look at Todd! He's on the tv again.* Finally, if you were to find your keys in your bed then you could say *I found them! They were in the bed.*

Denis: That's pretty clear now. So what other cases should I know about?

Geek: In addition to the cases we have been looking at, there are some other things to watch out for when it comes to the article. One thing is technical devices: we say on *the radio*, on *the phone*, on *the computer*, and on *the Internet*. Another thing is meals. In English there is no article with the words *breakfast, lunch* or *supper* when referring to the everyday meal. The same goes for holidays, languages and sports: we say *We celebrate Christmas, He speaks German, She plays ping pong,* et cetera. If I am referring to a specific holiday, however, I use an article: *That was the Christmas that Santa gave me a Playstation!* If I am referring to a specific supper event you also need to use the article, as in *Do you remember the supper for Andy's retirement last year?* Maybe

Lesson 9: Determiners – Part 1

next time we should rethink the idea of having an open bar. Also, with languages the article can be used when referring to the people who speak it, as in *I love the French. They are always in such a good mood!* It is also used when referring to a specific dialect: *Have you ever travelled the countryside in France? I had a hard time understanding the French in that region.*

Denis: Great. I've got it. One thing I don't get, however, is when to use articles with geographical places. For example, I know that you say the United States, but just Canada or Mexico. And with an ocean you use an article as in the Pacific Ocean, but with lakes you don't, as in Lake Superior. How can I know when to use an article?

Geek: Yes, I agree that that can be confusing. The first question you can ask yourself is 'Is the place plural?'. If so, then you usually need to use an article: the United States, the Great Lakes and the Netherlands are three examples. You have to be careful though as this rule of thumb does not work 100% of the time. We say Palm Springs and Thetford Mines.

Denis: O.k., that helps a bit. But most geographical entities don't end in an s. What do I do then?

Geek: Another question you can ask yourself is whether the geographical location has a clear boundary or outline. If so, then there is no article. This applies to cities, provinces and countries like New York, British Columbia, and Mexico. It also applies to parks, mountains, lakes and islands: Yellowstone, Mount Everest, Lake Michigan and Vancouver Island. It also applies to bays: Hudson Bay and Georgian Bay.

Denis: Okay, I follow so far.

Geek: On the other hand, places that don't have a clear, well-defined boundary or outline require an article. Places that are considered in this way include deserts, oceans, seas, valleys, coastlines and gulfs: the Sahara, the Pacific, the Baltic, the Fraser Valley and the Persian Gulf. Rivers are a trickier one: for rivers that are smaller and therefore more well-defined, there is no article: Trout River, Green River, etc. For the bigger ones, use an article: the St. Lawrence, the Nile, etc.

Denis: Okay then, so to sum up: clear outline, no article and no clear outline, article.

Geek: That's it. Now before we conclude for today, related to geography are roads, highways and streets. With roads and streets and avenues, they are well-defined stretches between two points and therefore do not take an article: Ring Road, Main Street, Electric Avenue, etc. With highways though, these are across long stretches and therefore not as easily defined so we say the TransCanada or the Interstate. The exception to this is where the highway is clearly identified by a number: we say Highway 401 or Route 70.

Denis: Alright.

Geek: And finally, although unrelated to geography, it is useful to know that there is no article with pages, chapters, gates, and rows when they are identified with a number. Thus we say Page One, Chapter Three, Gate 408, and Row 7.

Denis: Hey, the same goes for tables, too. I will often ask other servers for favours like 'Hey Jeff, could you take this to Table 3 for me? I don't say *the Table 3*.

Geek: Nice example! And unfortunately it looks like our time is up. Do you have any questions?

Denis: Nope, no questions from me. The boss is going to be here soon, so I need to go back to looking like I'm busy.

Geek: Good then. We have actually just barely scratched the surface of the determiners so we will continue with them tomorrow.

Denis: That sounds great. See you then!

Exercises, lesson 9

Part 1: Gap fill

Fill in the blanks with the correct article. Choose from the or Ø.

1. We are planning to travel to _____ North Africa next year. We want to see _____ Sahara desert, the pyramids of _____ Egypt and _____ Nile River.

2. In the seventies, more people who lived in _____ Quebec went to _____ church on _____ Sunday.

3. This summer I am going to _____ Great Lakes to do some camping. I really want to see _____ Lake Michigan.

Lesson 9: Determiners – Part 1

4. We are looking forward to seeing _____ Prairies and _____ Rockies when we cross Canada this summer. We want to vist the capitals too: _____ Winnipeg, _____ Regina and _____ Calgary.

5. The cruise to _____ Alaska leaves from _____ Seattle in _____ Washington. We will travel over _____ Pacific Ocean to _____ Vancouver Island and along _____ West Coast.

6. They are leaving on _____ Labour Day. They will fly to _____ California and then go by yacht down _____ East Coast, through _____ Caribbean, to _____ Jamaica.

7. She is studying _____ History at _____ University of Toronto. She is also learning how to speak _____ Spanish and _____ Italian.

8. We got tickets to see Megadeth. We will be in _____ Section 4, _____ Row 5, _____ Seats 21 and 22.

9. My parents like to play _____ sports in their spare time. My dad likes _____ golf and my mom likes _____ tennis.

10. We will take _____ Highway 86 down through _____ Eastern Townships to _____ United States. We can get onto _____ Interstate once we cross the border.

Part 2: Translation

Translate the following.

1. Il reste sur la rue des Pins.
2. Marc aime les sports. Il joue au hockey depuis deux ans.
3. N'oublie pas ton passeport quand tu iras en Chine.
4. Elle a lu le chapitre cinq jusqu'à la page 76.
5. Il va commencer l'école l'année prochaine.
6. Je crois que la liberté d'expression est une valeur fondamentale pour une société.
7. Généralement, il mange un bol de céréale au déjeuner. Au dîner, par contre, il mange comme un cochon.

8. – As-tu vu mes clés?
   – Je pense que tu les as laissées sur le lit ce matin.

9. L'événement aura lieu à l'intérieur de l'université demain à midi.

10. Il travaille sur l'ordinateur en ce moment. Il fait une recherche sur l'Internet.

Part 3: Contexts

Distinguish clearly between each of the following pairs of sentences by situating them in a context of at least 15 words each.

1. a) I love submarine sandwiches.
   b) I love the submarine sandwiches.

2. a) He is in college.
   b) He is in the college.

3. a) People are funny.
   b) The people are funny.

4. a) Ann is afraid of dobermans.
   b) Ann is afraid of the dobermans.

5. a) They were on T.V.
   b) They were on the T.V.

6. a) When is supper?
   b) When is the supper?

7. a) She needs money.
   b) She needs the money.

8. a) They were in church.
   b) They were in the church.

Lesson 10: Determiners – Part 2

Geek: Today we are going to continue talking about determiners. Are you ready?

Denis: You bet!

Geek: Let's begin with *this* and *that* and their plural forms *these* and *those*. First I want you to think back to our first encounter ten days ago. Do you remember what two notions I told you about which are fundamental to language?

Denis: Hmm. Ten days ago, eh? *Le temps passe vite!* Is there an expression like that in English?

Geek: Yes there is: Time flies when you're having fun. Here, I'll give you a hint: spatium and tempore.

Denis: Space and time! I remember now.

Geek: Good then. As you will see, these two notions come into play quite clearly with *this* and *that*.

Denis: Great. How so?

Geek: For starters, let's think about what I would say if I were to take a bottle of beer and put it in my hand. Would I say *This beer is delicious*, or *That beer is delicious*?

Denis: I think you would say *this beer*.

Geek: Right you are. In order to say *That beer is delicious*, where would the beer need to be?

Denis: Over there on the bar?

Geek: Right again. The speaker's choice comes down to the beer's proximity to him or her. *This* is used to signal that the object is inside his field, or *peripersonal space* as psychologists call it, while *that* signals that the object is outside of his field, or *extrapersonal space*.

Denis: Peripersonal and extrapersonal. Got it. So can you give me some more examples?

Geek: Think about these two: *I love this province* and *I love that province*. In which one is the subject living in the province he is referring to?

Denis: The first one, right?

Geek: Right, as in *I am living in Nova Scotia and I love this province. I don't plan to move from here anytime soon*. The second one would be said by a New Brunswicker talking about, let's say, Saskatchewan, as in *Saskatchewan? I love that province. One day I hope to live there*.

Denis: And become a Fransaskois! That's the term that the French people who live there call themselves there, did you know?

Geek: No, I did not.

Denis: I just noticed that with *this* you used *here* and with *that* you used *there*. I guess that makes sense since *here* means close to the speaker and *there* means far, right?

Geek: Good eye! You could be an English teacher yourself! Now in addition to space, *this* and *that* can also be used to make distinctions in terms of time. *This* associates things as being close to the speaker in time while *that* puts them further away, either back in the past or forward in the future. If I say *We chatted this morning* then you understand that we had our conversation today. If I say *We chatted that morning* then I am referring to a morning in the past: *Yes, I remember our conversation. It was a Wednesday I think. We chatted that morning for a few minutes and he never called again*. In addition I could say *This first year will be tough* or *That first year will be tough*. In the first one, I am referring to the year starting in the present. It could be said by a student starting his or her first year at college or university: *I just got my schedule and bought my books. This first year will be tough, I know, but people say that things get a bit easier in the second year once you get used to the place*. The second one could be said by a high school student who is thinking about the future: *I plan to go to university after I finish high school. I know that that first year will be tough but I think I have the perseverance required to succeed*.

Denis: Interesting. When I think back to when I first arrived here, I was far away from my friends and it was difficult. So I guess I could say *Those first few days were difficult*, right?

Lesson 10: Determiners – Part 2

Geek: Exactly.

Denis: So what else can you tell me?

Geek: In addition to the space and time dimension, the two articles can also be used on a psychological level too. One contrast is "This is what I think" and "That is what I think". In the former, the speaker is introducing something that is on his mind: *This is what I think. The restaurant needs a total makeover. We need to renovate, redo the menu, and lower prices.* In the latter, the speaker is referring back to something he already said and which is no longer on his mind: *This restaurant is a real dump. Would you like my opinion? We need to renovate, redo the menu, and lower prices. That is what I think.*

Denis: I see. One introduces, the other concludes. Neat.

Geek: Another similar case is something like *We had lunch at this great pub on Fifth Avenue.* and *We had lunch at that great pub on Fifth Avenue.* What does the second one tell you?

Denis: It tells me that I know what pub you are talking about.

Geek: Right , as in *I finally got together with Greg. We had lunch at that great pub on Fifth Avenue. Do you remember it? I mean the one you and I ate at last week.* In the first one, the speaker assumes that you don't know which pub he is talking about. It is on his mind and something he wants to talk about: *We had lunch at this great pub downtown. The service was great and the food fantastic. I can't remember the name of it though. I should take you there sometime.*

Denis: So the first time I met you, I could have said to my co-workers *This geeky English guy came in for beer this afternoon. Of course he ordered tea.* After they had seen you a few times, I could have said *That geeky English guy came in for breakfast this morning. You know, the one who always orders tea.*

Geek: Uh… yes.

Denis: Just checking!

Geek: So that's all I have to say about this and that. Let's move on to another common pair of determiners: *some* and *any*. For starters, the general rule is that *some* is used in affirmative contexts and *any* is reserved for negative statements and questions. We say *He wrote some e-mails, He didn't write any e-mails,* and *Did he write any e-mails*?

Denis: Alright. I guess this is where you say that the general rule doesn't always work?

Geek: Ha! Yesiree! You are getting to know me quite well. Of course, this rule is handy for beginners but too simple for more advanced speakers like yourself.

Denis: Fire away then.

Geek: Let's start with affirmative contexts. It would be perfectly fine to say *He bought some Star Wars memorabilia that was on E-Bay* or *He bought any Star Wars memorabilia that was on E-bay*. Do you see the difference?

Denis: Nope. I have no idea.

Geek: In the first one, I mean he bought a certain quantity: maybe it was figurines, t-shirts, a lunch box, or something else. In the second one, the impression is "if" or "no matter what it was": *Steve was a Star Wars nut. He bought any memorabilia that was there, any at all. It didn't matter if it was a t-shirt, a cup, underwear, he bought it. It drove his girlfriend crazy.*

Denis: Aah! Now I get it.

Geek: Let's look at negatives now. You could say *I didn't do some of the homework* just as you could say *I didn't do any of the homework*. In the former, I understand that you finished a portion of the homework whereas in the latter, I understand that you did none of it. Likewise, it is acceptable to say either *I don't like some songs by Celine Dion* or *I don't like any songs by Celine Dion*. In the former, you mean that there are some you like and some you don't. In the latter, you mean you dislike *all* of her songs.

Denis: Geez, you just described me...

Geek: Let's look at questions now and listen closely to this example as it applies to your line of work. It is perfectly fine to say *Would you like any dessert?* in the case where you have no idea whether or not the customer wants dessert. You are making the assumption that maybe they do, maybe they don't. You could say *Would you like some dessert?* if you have the impression that they do indeed want some. Maybe they mentioned they are still hungry or maybe they are looking at the desert menu and salivating.

Denis: Good to know in my line of work. So with *some*, you can say that you are more sure that the person wants dessert?

Lesson 10: Determiners – Part 2

Geek: Yes, you can. You are surer because there is something in the environment, some indication or clue, that is leading you to believe so. Another example would be *Did you eat some of my chips* and *Did you eat any of my chips*. In the first one, there are signs which are leading me to think that chips were consumed. Maybe I can see crumbs on your shirt or my chip bag is not as full as it was when I put it away in the cupboard. In the second one, I make no such assumption: maybe you did, maybe you didn't, as in *While I was out did you eat any of my chips? I left them out for you. Help yourself if you would like.*

Denis: Neat.

Geek: Having looked at some and any, let's move on to look at *each, every* and *all*. Each and every are used with count nouns only and can be interchanged in many contexts: *I clean my apartment each month* or *I clean my apartment every month*. Both sound o.k. to me. In cases where there are only two entities involved, only *each* is possible though: *There were houses on each side of the river.*

Denis: Two sides, got it. What about *all*?

Geek: *All* can be used with both count and non-count nouns. You can say *All homework must be submitted on time* or *All e-mails must be monitored*. Be careful with the verb that you use too: you can say *All of the information is important* but *All of the e-mails are deleted*. With a non-count noun you use a singular verb but with a plural count noun you use a plural verb.

Denis: I guess that applies to *some* too: *Some of the customers have arrived* but *Some of his advice is bad.*

Geek: Right you are. We can wrap up our discussion with the determiners *much, many, few,* and *little*. *Much* is used with non-count nouns: *I don't have much homework* or *Much wine was served*. *Many* is used with count nouns: *He has many friends* or *Did you see many people*? One other thing to note is that in affirmative sentences, *much* doesn't seem to be used as often. If you want to sound normal, use *a great deal of* or *a lot of*: *I have a lot of homework tonight.*

Denis: Or *a lot of wine* was served.

Geek: Right. Finally, *few* and *little*. You can use the former with count nouns as in *A few guys showed up*. The latter is used with non-count nouns: *A little progress was made.*

Denis: Hang on. Don't you say 'few' and 'little' sometimes? That is, with no 'a'?

Geek: Yes, we do, but it changes the tone of the sentence. The tone is more positive in *A few people showed up to help*. Here I am pleasantly surprised: maybe I was expecting no one to show up. The tone is more negative in the second one: *I was disappointed. Few people showed up. Maybe I should have advertised more.* The same goes for *We made a little progress* and *We made little progress*. In the former I am feeling proud but in the second I am feeling disappointed at the progress that was made: I was expecting more.

Denis: So I guess *a few* or *a little* is like saying *des* or *quelques* in French and *few* or *little* is like saying *peu de*.

Geek: Bingo. You are right on the money.

Denis: So is that it for today?

Geek: Yep. My phone has been vibrating for *a few minutes* so that means my wife and kids are getting impatient... again.

Denis: Great. I've got to get back to work. There are *a few* customers in here who probably have *little* patience with a waiter sitting down and talking about grammar!

Geek: Ha ha. I hereby dismiss you. Until tomorrow!

Denis: Until tomorrow!

Exercises, lesson 10

Part 1: Determiners review

Choose the correct determiner.

This/That/These/Those

1. – Hello, Bill. This/That is my friend Carl.
   – Nice to meet you, Carl.
2. This/That is what I need at the grocery store: butter, milk, eggs and oatmeal.
3. I don't know if I should wear these/those earrings here or these/those earrings over there.

Lesson 10: Determiners – Part 2

4. Look outside. Who is this/that person knocking on the door?
5. I remember the summer of 1989 clearly. This/That was the year I got my first car.
6. My car is making this/that strange sound again. Do you remember it?
7. I have this/that feeling in my knee. It's a strange tingling feeling that I have never felt before. Can you help me, Doc?
8. A sleeping bag, warm clothes, food and water. That/this is what we need to bring.

Some/Any

1. I had some/any trouble with my computer last night.
2. I apologize, sir. We don't have some/any extra chairs.
3. We didn't buy some/any of the books for our courses this year; only the less expensive ones.
4. She will no doubt have some/any advice for you.
5. Hey, why is my bottle almost empty? Did you drink some/any?
6. I like some/any of his paintings; just his early ones in fact.
7. Genevieve is an excellent skier who can stay in control on some/any kind of terrain.

Much/Many/Each/Every

1. The mayor had many/much things to say in the debate.
2. Does he speak much/many Spanish? We need a translator.
3. Did you have much/many trouble finding the classroom?
4. The police found clues in each/every of the two rooms.

Few/A Few/Little/A Little

1. A few/few people turned out to vote. We were disappointed.
2. A few/few students came to see me with questions. That was more than I expected.
3. Unfortunately the police have a little/little information at this point but as soon as they do, we will inform our viewers.

Part 2: Contexts

Distinguish clearly between each of the following pairs of sentences by situating them in a context of at least 15 words each.

1. a) This is my mom.
   b) That is my mom.

2. a) Give Tom this envelope.
   b) Give Tom that envelope.

3. a) This job is great.
   b) That job is great.

4. a) These shoes are comfortable.
   b) Those shoes are comfortable.

5. a) I will remember this year for the rest of my life.
   b) I will remember that year for the rest of my life.

6. a) This is how you send a text message.
   b) That is how you send a text message.

7. a) I didn't buy some of the items on your list.
   b) I didn't buy any of the items on your list.

8. a) The police arrested some protestors.
   b) The police arrested any protestors.

9. a) Do you need some help?
   b) Do you need any help?

10. a) A few people volunteered.
    b) Few people volunteered.

Lesson 11: Prepositions

Geek: Good afternoon once again Denis. How'r things today?

Denis: Hello Mr. G. Things are great. How about you?

Geek: All's well on my end too.

Denis: So what adventures did you have today? Anything exciting?

Geek: As a matter of fact, yes. I took a trip to Calgary to take in the Calgary Stampede.

Denis: Also known as "The Greatest Show on Earth". Awesome. If I can get some time off, I plan to check it out myself. I bet your kids had an awesome time. Uh… You took them, right?

Geek: Yeah yeah, I took them. And they had a great time: between the rodeo, the derby, the food, and the rides, I was surprised to see them still standing at the end of the day. The whole family's actually fast asleep up in our hotel room right now so I may be able to stay for an extra beer.

Denis: Well here's one to get you started. So what are we going to talk about today?

GEEK: Well today I thought we could talk about words like *in*, *on*, *at*, and *to*. Do you know what we call those words?

Denis: Prepositions?

Geek: Yes indeed.

Denis: Good. I know that I sometimes make mistakes with those words.

Geek: Yes, in my experience the prepositions can be one of the trickier areas to master. It might help to know that the prepositions fall into two categories. The first category is space, and the second category is… can you guess…?

Denis: Time!

Geek: Exactly. Let's begin with the spatial ones first. Let's start with the basic positional uses which you probably learned in school and with which you are no doubt familiar: *on* the box, *in* the box, *above* the box, *under* the box, *beside*, et cetera.

Denis: *Close to, next to, over, through*... yeah, I know those ones. I've only got one question though. I hear English people say *underneath* sometimes. How is that word different from *under*?

Geek: Good question. They both have basically the same meaning, however *under* is the one that we use the most. *Under* also has some abstract senses that *underneath* does not, like *He is under pressure* or *She was under the impression that I spoke German*. Underneath can also be used without an object, as in *They found something underneath*.

Denis: Great. I see.

Geek: Good. So where francophones usually run into difficulty is when talking about locations. Three prepositions that do this are *in*, *on*, and *at*. Here is what you need to remember: *In* has the idea of 'within a larger area' and is used with cities, countries, and continents: in Montreal, in Canada, in Asia. *On* is used when a surface is involved and therefore is used with planets, streets, highways, avenues, and coastlines: on Earth, on Main Street, on the TransCanada, on the North Shore.

Denis: Good. What about things like TV or the Internet? In French we say 'à la television' which is why I am always tempted to say 'at'. But I know that you say *on TV*.

Geek: Yes, technological devices are all used with *on*: on the Internet, on the radio, on the computer, on TV, or on the phone.

Denis: Got it. So what about *at*?

Geek: *At* is used for precise addresses or points: *I live at 2681 Bella Vista St.* or *I was at the bus stop*. It is also used to refer to targets as in *He aimed the gun at me* or *They were laughing at him*.

Denis: One problem that I have is remembering when to use *in* and *at* with a word like hotel. For instance, I could say *I'll see you in the hotel* or *I'll see you at the hotel*. In the former I specifically mean 'inside' the

Lesson 11: Prepositions

hotel. In the latter, the hotel is viewed as the point at which our rendez-vous will take place and does not specify whether I mean inside or outside. Right?

Geek: Right you are. And spoken like a true grammar geek! Now let's shift gears and look at these three prepositions in their temporal uses. *In* can be used with periods of time including years, months, times of the day and seasons: in 1987, in March, in the afternoon, in the winter. *On* is used with specific dates or days and holidays: on Sept. 11, on Sunday, on Labour Day, on Valentine's Day, on my birthday, etc. Finally, *at* is used for specific times of the day and also meals: at 12:30, or at supper.

Denis: Got it. What else can you tell me about prepositions?

Geek: One especially tricky one for francophones is *to*. Let me ask you this: how would you translate *Je vais au dépanneur* into English?

Denis: Hmm. I am going at the convenience store. No, wait... *to* the convenience store.

Geek: Exactly. Be careful there with *to*. Whenever the idea of movement involved, you need to make sure that you use *to*. Verbs which involve movement include *go, come, move, travel* and *run* and so we say He came *to* the party, They moved *to* California, We are traveling *to* Australia, or She ran *to* the scene. Contrary to *to*, *at* is used in more stationary contexts like I'll stay *at* home today, Wait *at* the corner, sit *at* the table, and so on.

Denis: Hmmm. That makes sense now. Doesn't the preposition *toward* also express the idea of movement? Like *to*?

Geek: Very good observation. Yes, that preposition expresses movement, but in a different way. Compare these two: *Pierre ran to the scene of the accident* and *Pierre ran towards the scene of the accident*. In only one of these is it implied that Pierre didn't reach the scene of the accident. The former or the latter?

Denis: The latter.

Geek: Right, as in *Pierre ran towards the scene of the accident but was intercepted by some police officers along the way. No one was allowed past the police barrier.* In the former, you could say something like *Pierre ran to the scene of the accident and was able to save a pregnant mother and her kids.*

Denis: What a hero!

Geek: Another preposition to be aware of is *by*: a sentence like *Saul will be done at nine* and *Saul will be done by nine* convey two different messages. In which one might Saul be done before nine o'clock?

Denis: The second one.

Geek: Right you are. In the first one, the speaker is saying that Saul will be done precisely at nine. In the second one, the speaker is saying that the latest time at which he will be done is nine. In other words, he could finish before that time, like at eight or eight-thirty.

Denis: O.k. Or as you English people like to say, okee-dokee!

Geek: The final set of prepositions that we can look at is *from, of, out of* and *off*. *From* is used with points of departure and also as the starting point of a process: *He ran from the monster, Wine is made from grapes*. It is often used with the preposition *to* as in *Kevin drove from B.C. to Quebec* or *Jerry works from nine to five*. *Of* is used to express cause, composition or source: *He died of cancer, It is made of wood, I am tired of her nagging*. *Off* has the meaning 'from the surface of' as in *Take the book off the table* and also 'down from' as in *Lionel fell off his horse*. *Out of* means 'from the interior': *He took it out of his pocket*.

Denis: Well, that clears up some questions that I had. What's next?

Geek: The next item we will talk about is verb-preposition combinations, or phrasal verbs as they are commonly called. Phrasal verbs are everywhere in English and incorporating them into your speech will go a long way towards making you sound like a native speaker. Take the word *get* for example. I can think of at least ten different possibilities.

Denis: Let me see... get along is one. There are get over, get out, get away. That's four that I can name.

Geek: You also have get through, get ahead, get by, get around, get down to and get into.

Denis: Geesh! How do you keep track of them all?

Geek: The phrasal verbs express two kinds of meaning: literal and non-literal. The literal ones are easier to understand. If I say *He ran out of the room screaming* then you understand that he exited the room running and screaming. If I say *Stand by the desk* then I am telling you to place yourself beside it.

Lesson 11: Prepositions

Denis: So far so good.

Geek: Non-literal meanings are more difficult to grasp because you can't decipher the meaning simply by looking at the individual parts. For instance, if I say *We have run out of hamburger buns*, there is no reference to an actual running movement like in the previous example. Here I mean that there is no more supply. Likewise, if I say that *I stand by my proposal* then I don't mean that I place myself beside it. I mean that I believe strongly in it.

Denis: O.k. Just one thing though: is it possible to say *We have run hamburger buns out of* or *I stand the proposal by*?

Geek: No, it is not, and you have just hit on the challenge with the phrasal verbs: knowing whether they are separable or inseparable, i.e. can an object be inserted between the verb and the preposition. In some cases, the phrasal verb can be both: I can say either *Write the number down* or *Write down the number*. It doesn't matter. But in the examples you mention, only *stand by the proposal* is possible, not *stand the proposal by*.

Denis: Yikes. Do you have any guidelines?

Geek: Yes, I do. First, if the verb is being used in its literal sense, then you don't separate: we say *He crossed over the bridge* or *They stepped on the bus* and never *He crossed the bridge over* or *They stepped the bus on*. Second, ask yourself whether there are three prepositions instead of two: phrasal verbs like *crack down on*, *get on with*, or *come down on* are all inseparable. Finally, ask yourself if there is a pronoun or not. If there is, then you must separate: *He broke it off*, *She turned him down*, et cetera. The only exceptions to this rule appear to be *into*: we say *The thieves broke into it* and not *The thieves broke it into*.

Denis: Phew! I'll try to remember all of that.

Geek: Before we close, since we are on the topic of prepositions I would like to mention some prepositional expressions which can cause francophones headaches. By prepositional expression I mean phrases like *interested in*, *afraid of*, *mad at*, et cetera. In a lot of cases, there is a correspondence between English and French. So if you say *J'ai peur de mon patron* then you say I am scared *of* my boss. If you say *Le film est basé sur une histoire vraie* then you say The movie is based *on* a true story.

Denis: That's not too hard. So when do the headaches start?

Geek: Where you need to take out the aspirin is in cases where English and French don't treat things the same way. For example, the sentence *Aline est responsable des horaires* would be translated not as *Aline is responsible of the schedules* but *for the schedules*. Likewise, in French you say *participer à, dépendre de, intéressé par*, and *semblable à*. In English we say participate *in*, depend *on*, interested *in* and similar *to* and not participate *at*, depend *of*, interested *by* or similar *at*. Big time no-no's.

Denis: Good to know. I will definitely watch myself in the future.

Geek: And on that note, we will have to conclude for today. Duty is calling once again.

Denis: No problem. Me too. So will I see you again tomorrow?

Geek: You will. Never fear, the Geek will be here!

Exercises, lesson 11

Part 1: Fill-in-the-blank

Supply the correct preposition: to, toward, at.

1. I will come _____ your house at 9:00 and leave _____ 10:00.
2. He aimed the gun right _____ his enemy and pulled the trigger.
3. They ran _____ the house but didn't make it.
4. They arrived _____ the train station this morning.
5. Why are they laughing _____ him?
6. Could you take this package _____ the post office? It must be mailed today.
7. They ran _____ the scene of the crime but were intercepted by the firemen.

Lesson 11: Prepositions

Supply the correct preposition: from, of, out of, off of, to.

1. He took a Kleenex _____ his pocket.
2. Take those papers _____ the secretary.
3. Wipe the dirt _____ the table.
4. She is tired _____ her job.
5. Johnny is always falling _____ his bike.
6. I borrowed the money _____ my sister and lent it _____ my brother.
7. He took the bus _____ Montreal and got there safe and sound.
8. I believe that she died _____ cancer.
9. Wine is made _____ grapes and whiskey is made _____ barley.
10. Could you get _____ the floor while I sweep it?
11. They walked all the way _____ downtown _____ their house.
12. He was in the hospital _____ January _____ June.
13. This house is made _____ wood and that one is made _____ brick.

Supply the correct preposition: at, in, on, for, since, by, to.

1. You will find our house _____ the end of the street.
2. She lives _____ an apartment on Laurier Boulevard.
3. The plane arrives _____ the morning _____ six o'clock.
4. You will find it more expensive living _____ British Columbia than _____ Quebec.
5. Look up _____ the top of the hill. They live _____ the castle and not _____ the valley.
6. I will meet you there _____ ten o'clock sharp.

115

The Grammar Geek

7. We will be done _____ five minutes.

8. I've been doing it _____ yesterday.

9. The family is gathering _____ Christmas.

10. I have thought about it _____ I was a little boy.

11. Hand in your assignments _____ tomorrow _____ five o'clock.

12. I have an appointment _____ Monday night _____ the evening.

13. The teacher will be in her office _____ 9:00 _____ noon.

14. He has been sick _____ the past three days.

15. He used to visit me _____ Sundays.

16. The order will be delivered _____ November 20th.

17. They have worked here _____ 2010.

18. I will meet with him _____ the morning.

19. My daughter is always either _____ her cell phone, _____ the computer, or surfing _____ the Internet.

20. Some people believe there is life _____ Mars.

21. I always seem to catch a cold _____ the winter.

22. Wait for me _____ the corner. I will be there _____ 7:00 and not a moment before.

23. My birthday falls _____ a Monday this year. I always get a lot of presents _____ my birthday.

24. You need to submit your application _____ this Friday at the latest.

25. They are planning to move _____ New Brunswick.

26. We live _____ Oak Avenue, _____ 1418 to be precise.

27. They intend to travel all the way _____ the North Pole.

Lesson 11: Prepositions

Supply the correct preposition: under, underneath.

1. They found some artifacts _____ the rocks.

2. They moved the rocks and found something _____.

3. You father is _____ a lot of stress these days.

4. He is good at working _____ pressure.

Part 2: Phrasal verbs

For each pair of sentences, determine which one has a literal use (L) of a phrasal verb and which one has a non-literal use (NL). For the non-literal use, find a close synonym.

Exemple: Jan put the straw up the pipe. **L**
They needed a place to stay so we put them up. **NL:** *accommodate*

1. He turned down the wrong street and got lost.
   The company turned down the offer.

2. Could you carry these things out of the room?
   We will need more supplies to carry out the mission.

3. People should stand up for their beliefs.
   Everybody stood up when the president entered.

4. The police will look into the case.
   The kids looked into the pond and saw the fish.

5. They got across the bridge.
   How can I get my point across better?

6. The lawyer went ahead with his opening statement.
   Andrea's name was called first so she went ahead of me.

7. They got through the tunnel and to the other side.
   It was a difficult time but they got through it.

Replace the italicized phrasal verb in each sentence with a verb from the list below.

Discover	Disappoint	Consider	Discuss
Make sense	Interrupt	Delay	Appear
Resemble	Cancel	Avenge	Quit
Obey	Leave	Examine	Create
Reduce	Support	Enter illegally	Conduct

1. They had to *cut down on* their expenses.
2. The boss is going to *think over* your idea.
3. He *takes after* his father, not his mother.
4. Please *look over* the document for any mistakes.
5. They had to *call off* the parade due to rain.
6. Your mother and I will *talk* it *over*.
7. When no one was looking he *slipped out*.
8. How many people are going to *show up* tonight?
9. The flight was *held up* for an hour due to bad weather.
10. It is not very polite to *cut in* when someone is talking.
11. The lawyer *backed up* his arguments with facts.
12. Researchers are going to *carry out* a study.
13. To be a member you need to *abide by* the rules.
14. Someone *broke into* my house last night.
15. The police are trying to *figure out* how the thief did it.
16. The test was so long that the student *gave up*.
17. He *made up* a story and lied to his parents.
18. I know exactly how to *get back at* him for hurting you.
19. The facts did not *add up* so the hypothesis was rejected.
20. The team played poorly and *let down* the fans.

Part 3: Combinations

Translate the following using the adjective or verb in brackets. Use a dictionary if necessary.

1. J'ai peur des coquerelles. (afraid)
2. Je m'excuse d'avoir oublié. (sorry)
3. Il est fâché contre moi. (mad)
4. Il est intéressé par le sujet. (interested)
5. On ne croit pas aux ovnis. (believe)
6. Qui est responsable des nouveaux employés? (responsible)
7. Je cherche de l'assistance. (look)
8. Elle ne connaît pas le logiciel. (be familiar)
9. Cette robe est différente de celle-là. (different)
10. Ce candidat est semblable à l'autre. (be similar)
11. L'équipe va participer aux séries éliminatoires. (participate)
12. Il est sûr de son choix. (sure)
13. Ils sont fiers de leurs enfants. (proud)
14. Je vais payer ton épicerie cette semaine. (pay)
15. Cela va dépendre de lui. (depend)

Lesson 12: Sentence Structure

Denis: So Mr. Geek, what are we going to discuss today? And is today our last lesson?

Geek: Sadly, it is my dear Denis. The family and I will be shipping out tomorrow morning. And quite honestly I think the wife and kids are looking forward to moving on and getting back to home sweet home.

Denis: So what is 'on deck' today as you English people like to say?

Geek: Well up until now our focus has been on the various parts of speech: nouns, verbs, adjectives, adverbs, prepositions, determiners, and so on. These items are the building blocks of what we are going to finish with: the sentence.

Denis: The sentence! I am ready.

Geek: So like I said, words are the building blocks of sentences. They are what we learn first as children in fact: Mama, Dada, soother, milk, poo-poo, and so on. As we get older, we begin to put words together to form sentences, first as *Me want water* and *Me go poo-poo* and later as more complex sentences like *I would love it if you poured me a glass of water please Sir* and *I have to use the bathroom*. There are some other… ahem… less polite ways of saying that latter one which you have probably picked up on listening to your English friends.

Denis: Yeah, in French we have less polite ways of saying that too!

Geek: So then, moving along. The first thing I want to discuss is how sentences can be of different kinds of 'voice'. In English there are two kinds: active and passive. An active sentence is something like *Ron ate a taco* and a passive sentence is something like *A taco was eaten by Ron*. Do you see the difference?

Denis: Yep, I sure do. In the active one, the focus seems to be on Ron and the fact that he ate a taco. In the passive one, the focus is on a taco getting eaten.

Geek: Indeed. The active voice focuses on the *doer* of the action while the passive voice focuses more on *what is done*. The passive voice is composed of two parts: the correct form of the verb *to be* and the past participle. In some cases, like my taco example, there is a phrase with 'by', but it is not always needed. Sometimes the doer is obvious or unknown as in *It is believed that Bigfoot roams the Kootneys* or *The money was stolen*.

Denis: Sounds good. But you said I need to have the right form of be. What do you mean?

Geek: Let's take the verb *google* and put it in the passive with the various verb tenses: It *is* googled, It *was* googled, It *is being* googled, It *was being* googled, It *has been* googled, It *had been* googled. Then there are the modals: It *will be* googled, It *can be* googled, et cetera[1].

Denis: Good. I see now.

Geek: What I want to discuss next are interrogative and non-interrogative sentence forms. Interrogative forms, or 'question' forms as some people refer to them, are done quite differently in English which is why French speakers have a lot of difficulty being accurate in this area.

Denis: I used to always get mixed up between *do*, *does* and *did*. I have friends who don't use them properly either. They say things to customers like *When do you arrive in Banff?* when they should say *When did you arrive in Banff?*

Geek: Yes, that is definitely a big no-no, as is eliminating the auxiliary altogether and saying *When you arrive?*. So what do you need to remember? Well there are two kinds of question forms: yes-no questions and information questions. There are also two formulae which can help you out. The first is ASVOR: auxiliary + subject + verb + object + rest. For a yes-no question you always start with the auxiliary, followed by the subject, the verb, the object, and whatever is left over. For example, *Do you like pizza with mushrooms on it? Does he like pizza with mushrooms on it?* And *Did they like pizza with mushrooms on it?*

Denis: I see. And you can give a short answer, right? Like *Yes, I do, Yes, he does* or *Yes, they did*.

---

[1] A chart outlining the active and passive forms is included in the Reference Section.

Lesson 12: Sentence Structure

Geek: Exactly. Or *No, I don't, No, he doesn't*, or *No, they didn't*. Now, the exception to this little formula is when you are using the verb *to be*. We say *Was he at the party?* or *Are they in the room?* Here there is no *do, does*, or *did*.

Denis: Got it.

Geek: Now for the second kind of question: the information question. The formula that you need to remember is QuASVOR: you always start with the question word, followed by the auxiliary, subject, verb, object and the rest so we say *When do you put the garbage out on the street? Why did he put the garbage out on the street?* and *Where does he leave the keys every morning?*

Denis: Hang on a minute. Don't you sometimes say *Who told him?* or *Who took it?* There is no auxiliary there.

Geek: Yes, we do say those. In my previous sentences I was asking about the object, not the subject. Take for example a sentence like *My girlfriend texts me all the time*. If I want to know about the object of the taking, i.e. who your girlfriend texts all the time, then I say *Who does your girlfriend text all the time*; that is, the auxiliary is required. If I would like to know about *who* is doing the texting, i.e. the subject of the sentence, then I say *Who texts you all the time?*; no auxiliary required.

Denis: I see. Object, auxiliary; Subject, no auxiliary.

Geek: The formulae ASVOR and QuASVOR also work with modal auxiliaries and so you get *When should Maria tell the boss about it?* or *Can Sylvie come to the party?*

Denis: Those are handy formulae. I am constantly asking my customers questions so I'll have lots of opportunity to practice!

Geek: The final thing I'll mention about questions pertains to what we call tags. In English, we add a tag onto a statement when we are looking to confirm its veracity. For example, You have a gerbil, *don't you*? Or You took the bus, *didn't you*?

Denis: Yeah! English people do that all the time. We do it in French too. We say 'n'est-ce pas' a lot, as in *Tu aimes lire, n'est-ce pas?* or *tu as lu le livre, n'est-ce pas?*

Geek: You do. The thing you need to remember with tags is that when the main verb is affirmative, your tag is negative and when the main verb is negative, your tag is positive. You also need to add an auxiliary do, does, or did and always use a pronoun. So here are three statements. *They go to the movies, She goes to the movies,* and *We went to the movies.* Try those.

Denis: They go to the movies, don't they?

Geek: Yep.

Denis: She goes to the movies, doesn't she?

Geek: Yep.

Denis: We went to the movies, didn't we?

Geek: Right again. The exception to this little pattern, once again, is the verb *to be.* So if I say *We are teachers, She's a teacher,* and *They were teachers,* the tags are *We are teachers, aren't we, She's a teacher, isn't she* and… care to take a shot at the third one…?

Denis: They were teachers, weren't they? No problemo!

Geek: Great. Now that we have covered the gamut of interrogative sentences, let's move along and look at affirmative ones. First off, there are some terms that are essential to know: phrase, dependent clause, and independent clause. A phrase is a group of two or more words which form an idea. It does not contain a subject or a verb; for example: at the bank, every day, last night, in the beginning, et cetera. An independent clause is also a group of words but unlike a phrase it contains a subject and a verb and conveys a complete thought. For example, *I had good marks* or *We enjoy sitting by the fireplace.* Finally, a dependent clause is a group of words but does not express a complete thought. It consists of a subordinate conjunction, a subject and a verb. For example: *whenever I come here, because we had bad marks,* or *while you are waiting.* None of these groups of words can stand on their own; they require another clause to complete the idea.

Denis: I see.

Geek: So if you want to make your English more refined and native-speaker-like, there are a few things that you can do. First of all, you can vary your sentence structure by using subordinate conjunctions. The subordinate conjunctions can be broken down into several

Lesson 12: Sentence Structure

categories according to the relationship they evoke. Some denote cause and effect like *because, as, so that,* and *since*. Some denote time: *after, before, since[2], until, when, whenever, as soon as.* Some denote contrast: *whereas, however, although, even though, while.* Finally, some denote condition: *if, even if, only if, as if, provided that, as long as,* and *unless.*

Denis: That's quite a long list to choose from. I'll bet you really impress the ladies with those. Heh heh.

Geek: Another thing you can do to improve your English, especially when writing but in speaking too, is to combine independent clauses. One could say *Denis worked hard. He got the promotion* but this sounds a bit choppy.

Denis: Choppy?

Geek: Choppy... as in rough, or unsmooth. In order to smooth things out, you can use a coordinating conjunction and say *Denis worked hard and he got the promotion* or *He worked hard so he got the promotion.* The complete list of coordinating conjunctions includes *for, and, nor, but, or, yet, so.*

A third way to make your English sound better is to use what is called an adverb conjunction. Some are used when adding information, like *additionally, furthermore,* or *moreover.* Some denote contrast, as in *despite, otherwise, however,* or *nevertheless.* Some denote time: *eventually, finally, meanwhile, subsequently.* They also can be used to illustrate or add emphasis: *indeed, above all, for example, for instance, namely.* Finally, some denote result or consequence: *consequently, accordingly, instead, hence, therefore* and *thus.*

Denis: That's quite the list to remember.

Geek: It's a question of practice, as usual. They can come at the beginning of a clause, as in *Above all, employees must be polite.* You can also make your writing look better by using one of these conjunctions with a semi-colon as in *Donald Trump is incredibly smart; moreover, he is incredibly handsome*!

Denis: Eee... I don't know about that!

---

[2] Note the different uses of *since* : *I have lived here since I was born* (time) and *Since he didn't have any money, he had to borrow some* (cause and effect).

Geek: Now before we conclude this our final lesson, there are a few other items that I'd like to mention. First up is the comma splice. One common thing for French speakers to do is to combine two independent clauses with a comma and so they will do something like *She worked hard, she got good marks*. This is a big no-no: you need to combine these statements with a conjunction.

Denis: So I could say *She worked hard <u>and</u> she got good marks* or <u>Because</u> *she worked hard, she got good marks*.

Geek: Exactly. Second up is the run-on. You need to avoid saying, or more often writing, something like *She got good marks she worked hard*. This is called a run-on sentence because one clause runs into the other.

Denis: O.k. So I could use *and* or *because* again.

Geek: Yes. Now then, the third item I need to discuss is the relative clause. Relative clauses fall into two categories: restrictive and non-restrictive, or as some grammarians like to say essential and non-essential. A restrictive clause contains information that limits the thing to which the person is referring. For example, *I spoke with a man who had seven kids* or *The hammer which was on sale looked like the best deal*. In these two cases the relative clauses *who had seven kids* and *which was on sale* are essential in order to understand who or what the speaker is referring to. A non-restrictive clause, on the other hand, contains information that does not restrict the scope of the thing referred to. It is separated with a comma in written English; for example, *I spoke with a man, who had seven kids* or *The house, which people believed was haunted, was put up for sale by its owners*.

Denis: I see. One thing I have always wondered about is when to use *who*, when to use *which* and when to use *that*. And what about *whose*?

Geek: Right. In other words, how to know which relative pronoun to pick. *Who* and *which* are quite straightforward: the former is used to refer to people, the latter to refer to things. *Whose* is used to indicate that the noun following it belongs to or is associated with the noun preceding it, *I once met a man whose name was Boris* or the famous line *Mary had a little lamb whose face was white as snow*. *That* can be used for either things or people but one thing you need to note is that *that* can't be used in a non-restrictive way. It would be ungrammatical to say *The coat, that was hanging on the hook, was brown*. Here you would need to use *which*.

Lesson 12: Sentence Structure

Denis: Easy as pie. And what about *whom*? I hear that sometimes. Did you ever hear the Metallica song *For whom the bell tolls?*

Geek: Heh heh. No, but I have read Earnest Hemingway's novel from which the title was obviously taken. Hemingway got the title from the famous English poet John Donne. I assume you have heard of these two English icons?

Denis: Hemingway yes, Donne no.

Geek: Well one out of two isn't bad... I can forgive you. So like in your song title, *whom* is used with a preposition: The person *for whom* the bell tolls. You can also say *The girl to whom I am talking* or *The person with whom I am going*. These tend to sound a bit too formal and pretentious though. Normally speakers say *The girl I am talking to* or *The person who I am going with*.

Denis: Good. So if I want to sound normal, which I do, then I will stick with the second ones!

Geek: Good plan.

Denis: So what else do I need to know?

Geek: I'm afraid that's it. We are done. Terminado.

Denis: Terminado?

Geek: Terminado.

Denis: Shucks, well I guess it was inevitable that this moment would arrive. Thanks a lot for all that you have taught me Mr. Syme. I have really enjoyed our grammar lessons together and being your "apprenti".

Geek: It has been my pleasure, *apprentice*. You know, when we first started our lessons a couple of weeks ago, you said that you wanted to learn more about the English language to make you a more fluent and accurate speaker. I have no doubt that your goal has been accomplished. I mean look at how beautifully you just used the present perfect.

Denis: Hey you're right! And I didn't even realize it.

Geek: That, *mon ami*, is a sign that you are becoming more and more like a native speaker. Consciously you probably won't remember a lot of what we discussed but unconsciously you will and it will show in the way you use the language as time goes by.

Denis: Actually, to be honest, I don't think that remembering will be a problem. I didn't tell you, but I have been secretly recording our grammar lessons the whole time on my cellphone. Ha! I'll be able to listen to them again and again.

Geek: What a great idea! You will definitely want to hang on to that. Feel free to share it with whomever you would like… I hereby waive all of my rights to any potential profits. Ha ha.

Denis: Seriously though, I *know* that my English has improved since we met. And to show you my gratitude for all that you showed me, I got you *un petit quelque chose*.

Geek: Oh really? A little something for me? You shouldn't have.

Denis: Here you go. It's a genuine leather cowboy hat. With your name on it… your nickname, not your real one.

Geek: Wow! Thanks a lot Denis. What a great-looking hat. Actually, do you want to know something funny?

Denis: What?

Geek: Well to celebrate your "graduation", I got you something too…

Denis: Oh yeah? Cool. What did you get me?

Geek: Surprise, it's a hat! Well it's more like a helmet I guess. Here. It's one of those tacky tourist hats that lets you carry two beer cans on each side. You connect them to your mouth with this plastic tube straw.

Denis: Awesome!! I always wanted one of those!

Geek: Congratulations. I hereby declare you the first graduate of the Grammar Geek's School of Language.

Denis: Wow! Thank-you Mr. G. It's even got my name on it. I can't wait to try it out with my buddies tonight!

Geek: And I can't wait to show off my new hat to my kids. They are going to get a kick out of it. Say, why don't you pour each of us one last beer so that we can celebrate together?

Lesson 12: Sentence Structure

Denis: Great idea. I can use my new hat! On second thought, I'll just use a glass. There are customers starting to come in.

Geek: How about a toast?

Denis: That would be a fitting way to end things.

Geek: Let us raise our glasses. Here's to a long life and a happy one, a quick death and an easy one, a good friend and an honest one, a cold pint… and another one!

Denis: Ha ha. I will drink to that.

Geek: Cheers to grammar!

Denis: And cheers to the Grammar Geek!

Exercises, lesson 12

Part 1: Active and passive voice

Transform the following sentences from the passive to the active voice. In some cases it is necessary to supply a subject.

1. The bus was taken by Henry.
2. All meals are prepared by the head chef.
3. The turkey was cut by my Dad.
4. The home has been inspected by him.
5. The truck is being loaded by the men.
6. Coffee is served all day.
7. The course is given by two teachers.
8. The car has been repaired by the mechanic.
9. The speaker was being introduced by Anna.
10. The thief had been arrested by the police.

Transform the following sentences from the active to the passive voice. In some cases it is necessary to supply a subject.
1. He signed the contract.
2. The doorman opens the door.
3. The buyer is considering my offer.
4. Harold was feeding the fish.
5. Jake has written several books.
6. Three players scored a goal.
7. The committee changed the company's policy.
8. The boss had already fired three employees.
9. The thieves stole the jewelry upstairs.

Use the correct voice of the verb in parentheses.
1. People (surprise) by the snowstorm yesterday.
2. All of my friends (like) the movie last night.
3. English (teach) every evening next fall.
4. The protest (happen) downtown at this moment.
5. Wilson (borrow) the money from me two weeks ago.
6. Tom and Lucy (work) at this company for six years.
7. Davis (promote) to the position of Assistant Manager this morning.
8. More German courses (offer) at our school next year.
9. Several employees (hire) since the beginning of the year.
10. The kids (spoil) by their parents when they were little.
11. If you think hard, I am sure you (remember) his name.
12. Jane (drive) to Toronto when the car ran out of gas.
13. This bank (found) in 1908 by my great, great grandfather.
14. The teacher (present) some interesting remarks when I came in the class.
15. The guests (introduce) to everyone at the moment.
16. The report (examine) by a committee this morning.

Lesson 12: Sentence Structure

Part 2: Question forms

Make yes/no questions with the following sentences. Also make tag questions.

1. Fred drives carefully.
2. They study every evening.
3. She buys a new dress.
4. Mr. Harper walked downtown with his friend.
5. The students in that class always work hard.
6. Mr. Williams meets them on Fridays.
7. Tom's friend finished all of the work.
8. Miss Stewart is wearing a dress.
9. Peter does his homework.
10. The two plumbers did the work.
11. André always comes on time.
12. Miss Cunningham paid the bill.
13. Everyone understands the last two questions.
14. The students have trouble with question forms.
15. John is coming tonight.

Make wh- questions based on the underlined elements. Also make tag questions.

1. Alice goes <u>to the movies</u> every Thursday.
2. Miss Peters is writing <u>those letters</u>.
3. Bill's birthday is <u>on the twelfth of August.</u>
4. There are <u>twenty-one</u> floors in that building.
5. They spend two weeks <u>in Florida.</u>
6. Chuck is coughing <u>because he has a bad cold.</u>
7. <u>The Browns</u> left at six o'clock.
8. The students studied <u>the irregular verbs.</u>

9. Brian has <u>two thousand dollars</u>.
10. There were <u>fourteen</u> guests at the party.
11. Mr. Burke bought <u>his new car</u> last Saturday.
12. Oka is <u>ninety miles</u> from there.
13. <u>Their classes</u> usually begin at nine o'clock.
14. I'm going <u>because the speech will be interesting</u>.
15. That customer wants <u>four packs of cigarettes</u>.
16. Dorothy wore <u>the pink dress</u>.
17. We call those things <u>"gadgets"</u> in English.
18. <u>My friends</u> helped me move yesterday afternoon.
19. Mr. Wilson gave the annual report <u>to Mr. Johnson</u>.
20. The whole trip takes <u>about twenty hours</u>.
21. We're going to look for winter coats <u>at that store</u>.
22. Those dictionaries belong to <u>Jean-Claude</u>.
23. Our friends stayed in California <u>for two weeks</u>.
24. The messenger gave <u>the mail</u> to Mr. Johnson.
25. The word "rapid" means <u>"fast" or "quick"</u>.

Part 3: Sentence structure[3]

Indicate the relationship between clauses in the following sentences: cause/effect, time, contrast or condition.

1. George was texting while driving *even though it is illegal*.
2. You can come *whenever you feel like it*.
3. I won't go to university *unless I get a scholarship*.
4. *While I think it is a good idea*, I don't propose to go through with it.
5. We'll have to improvise *since we don't have all the ingredients*.
6. I can watch your cat *until you return*.

---

[3] For a summary of the various conjunctions, see the charts in the Reference Section.

Lesson 12: Sentence Structure

7. He can move over *so that you have room to sit.*
8. Come to see me *if you need some assistance.*
9. He takes the bus *where as I ride my bike.*
10. No one is available to work *as everyone is on strike.*

Circle the best answer.

1. _____ the snow storm, classes will go on as usual.
    a) Because
    b) However
    c) Although
    d) Despite

2. _____ he is not very smart, he has still had a lot of success.
    a) Even
    b) In spite of
    c) Even though
    d) Provided that

3. _____ the requirements, I was not accepted into the Police Technology program.
    a) Because of
    b) Since
    c) Because
    d) Even if

4. Stephan loves his poutine with peas on it _____ I like it with chicken.
    a) Whereas
    b) Whenever
    c) So that
    d) Therefore

5. Nurses need to have extensive training _____ they are prepared for the job.

    a) So that

    b) Whenever

    c) Only if

    d) As long as

6. Nancy completed all of her homework assignments. _____, she got an A for the course.

    a) Instead

    b) Meanwhile

    c) Consequently

    d) On the contrary

7. The professor refused to allow me to redo the test _____ I produced a doctor's note.

    a) In spite of

    b) Even

    c) Since

    d) Unless

8. I was feeling quite sick yesterday. _____ how I felt, I did the exam.

    a) Moreover

    b) In spite of

    c) Namely

    d) Whenever

Improve the structure of the following sentences by combining clauses. More than one combination may be possible.

1. He studies hard. He gets great marks.

2. Travis is sick, he can't come to the meeting.

3. The chili was too spicy. I didn't go back for a second helping.

Lesson 12: Sentence Structure

4. We finished class early. We went out for drinks.
5. She handed in her assignment, she went home to sleep.
6. He was ill. He still finished his PhD.
7. Jody was the top student in the class. He received an award.
8. Caroline handed in her homework late. She lost points.
9. The student wrote a provocative essay. It was full of spelling mistakes.
10. He submitted his application. He knew his chances of getting the job were low.
11. Tom worked at the manufacturing plant. His wife Tara stayed at home with their twin daughters.
12. You can come with me. Don't embarrass me again like you did last time.

Complete the sentence with <u>that</u>, <u>who</u>, <u>which</u> or <u>whom</u>.

1. The guy _____ is talking to Gary is my friend.
2. We met someone _____ name was Jane.
3. The box, _____ was quite heavy, fell on my head.
4. The homework _____ the teacher gave us was easy this time.
5. The person to _____ you are speaking is his brother.
6. I work for a company _____ develops marketing strategies.
7. He found the woman _____ had saved his life.
8. Is that the man _____ dog bit your leg?
9. The new employee, _____ was hired yesterday, will be starting soon.
10. With _____ am I speaking?

11. We need to know the number of products _____ are sold.

12. Business Ethics, _____ is typically taught in the second year, is a mandatory course.

13. This is a very lightweight computer _____ you can easily carry with you on the plane.

14. The guy against _____ I am boxing has never been defeated.

15. He has lost everything _____ he worked so hard for.

Reference Section

Simple Present

Affirmative	Negative	Interrogative
I serve	I don't serve	Do I serve?
You serve	You don't serve	Do you serve?
He/She/It serves	He/she/it doesn't serve	Does he/she/it serve?
We serve	We don't serve	Do we serve?
They serve	They don't serve	Do they serve?

Present Progressive

Affirmative	Negative	Interrogative
I am ('m) serving	I am ('m) not serving	Am I serving?
You are ('re) serving	You are ('re) not serving	Are you serving?
He/She/It is ('s) serving	He/She/It is ('s) not serving	Is he/she/it serving?
We are ('re) serving	We are ('re) not serving	Are we serving?
They are ('re) serving	They are ('re) not serving	Are they serving?

Simple Past

Affirmative	Negative	Interrogative
I served	I didn't serve	Did I serve?
You served	You didn't serve	Did you serve?
He/She/It served	He/she/it didn't serve	Did he/she/it serve?
We served	We didn't serve	Did we serve?
They served	They didn't serve	Did they serve?

Past Progressive

Affirmative	Negative	Interrogative
I was serving	I was not (wasn't) serving	Was I serving?
You were serving	You were not (weren't) serving	Were you serving?
He/She/It was serving	He/She/It was not (wasn't) serving	Was he/she/it serving?
We were serving	We were not (weren't) serving	Were we serving?
They were serving	They were not (weren't) serving	Were they serving?

Future: Will

Affirmative	Negative	Interrogative
I will ('ll) serve	I will not (won't) serve	Will I serve?
You will ('ll) serve	You will not (won't) serve	Will you serve?
He/She/It will ('ll) serve	He/she/it will not (won't) serve	Will he/she/it serve?
We will ('ll) serve	We will not (won't) serve	Will we serve?
They will ('ll) serve	They will not (won't) serve	Will they serve?

Future: Be going to

Affirmative	Negative	Interrogative
I am going to serve	I am not going to serve	Am I going to serve?
You are going to serve	You are not going to serve	Are you going to serve?
He/She/It is going to serve	He/she/it is not going to serve	Is he/she/it going to serve?
We are going to serve	We are not going to serve	Are we going to serve?
They are going to serve	They are not going to serve	Are they going to serve?

Present Perfect

Affirmative	Negative	Interrogative
I have ('ve) served	I have not (haven't) served	Have I served?
You have ('ve) served	You have not (haven't) served	Have you served?
He/She/It has ('s) served	He/She/It has not (hasn't) served	Has he/she/it served?
We have ('ve) served	We have not (haven't) served	Have we served?
They have ('ve) served	They have not (haven't) served	Have they served?

Present Perfect Progressive

Affirmative	Negative	Interrogative
I have ('ve) been serving	I have not (haven't) been serving	Have I been serving?
You have ('ve) been serving	You have not (haven't) been serving	Have you been serving?
He/She/It has ('s) been serving	He/She/It has not (hasn't) been serving	Has he/she/it been serving?
We have ('ve) been serving	We have not (haven't) been serving	Have we been serving?
They have ('ve) been serving	They have not (haven't) been serving	Have they been serving?

Past Perfect Progressive

Affirmative	Negative	Interrogative
I had ('d) been serving	I had not (hadn't) been serving	Had I been serving?
You had ('d) been serving	You had not (hadn't) been serving	Had you been serving?
He/She/It had ('d) been serving	He/She/It had not (hadn't) been serving	Had he/she/it been serving?
We had ('d) been serving	We had not (hadn't) been serving	Had we been serving?
They had ('d) been serving	They had not (hadn't) been serving	Had they been serving?

Past Perfect

Affirmative	Negative	Interrogative
I had ('d) served	I had not (hadn't) served	Had I served?
You had ('d) served	You had not (hadn't) served	Had you served?
He/She/It had ('d) served	He/She/It had not (hadn't) served	Had he/she/it served?
We had ('d) served	We had not (hadn't) served	Had we served?
They had ('d) served	They had not (hadn't) served	Had they served?

Future Perfect

Affirmative	Negative	Interrogative
I will ('ll) have served	I will ('ll) not have served	Will I have served?
You will ('ll) have served	You will ('ll) not have served	Will you have served?
He/She/It will ('ll) have served	He/She/It will ('ll) not have served	Will he/she/it have served?
We will ('ll) have served	We will ('ll) not have served	Will we have served?
They will ('ll) have served	They will ('ll) not have served	Will they have served?

Future Perfect Progressive

Affirmative	Negative	Interrogative
I will ('ll) have been serving	I will ('ll) not have been serving	Will I have been serving?
You will ('ll) havebeen serving	You will ('ll) not have been serving	Will you have been serving?
He/She/It will ('ll) have been serving	He/She/It will ('ll) not have been serving	Will he/she/it have been serving?
We will ('ll) have been serving	We will ('ll) not have been serving	Will we have been serving?
They will ('ll) have been serving	They will ('ll) not have been serving	Will they have been serving?

Verbs which can express both actions and states

Verb	State Use	Action Use
have	Do you have a dog?	We are having supper. She is having a baby. We are having problems.
be	He is funny.	He is being funny.
feel	How does she feel?	They are feeling the effects.
weigh	It weighs ten kilograms.	Bert is weighing the apples.
taste	This tastes great.	I am tasting the sauce.
hear	Did you hear that noise?	The priest is hearing confessions.
smell	Your cake smells good.	Why are you smelling my cake?

Verb	State Use	Action Use
look	She looks good today.	Are you looking at the screen?
see	Did you see the sign?	She is seeing a doctor about it. He is seeing a new girl now.
sound	That sounds like a siren.	The alarm is sounding.
think	I think you are wrong.	They are thinking about it.
mind	I don't mind.	I was minding my own business.

Modals: Translations

Je peux le faire.	I can do it.
Je pourrais le faire.	I could do it.
Je pouvais le faire.	I could do it.
J'ai pu le faire.	I was able to do it.
Je pourrai le faire.	I will be able to do it.
Je vais pouvoir le faire.	I am going to be able to do it.
Il se peut que je le fasse.	I may/might do it.
Je dois le faire.	I must/have to do it.
Je devrais le faire.	I should do it.
J'ai dû le faire.	I had to do it. I must have done it.
Je devrai le faire.	I will have to do it.
Je vais devoir le faire.	I am going to have to do it.

Conjunctions

Coordinating Conjunctions
for, and, nor, but, or, yet, so.

Subordinate Conjunctions

Cause/Effect	Time	Contrast	Condition
because	after	whereas	if
as	before	however	even if
so that	since	although	only if
since	until	even though	as if
	when	while	as long as
	whenever		unless
	as soon as		provided that

Adverb Conjunctions

Addition	Contrast	Time
additionally	despite	eventually
furthermore	in spite of	finally
moreover	otherwise	meanwhile
in addition	however	subsequently
also	nevertheless	

Illustration/Emphasis	Result
indeed	consequently
above all	accordingly
for example	instead
for instance	hence
namely	therefore
	thus

Active and Passive Voice

Active	Passive
He serves lunch.	Lunch is served (by him).
He is serving lunch.	Lunch is being served (by him).
He served lunch.	Lunch was served (by him).
He was serving lunch.	Lunch was being served (by him).
He has served lunch.	Lunch has been served (by him).
He had served lunch.	Lunch had been served (by him).
He is going to serve lunch.	Lunch is going to be served (by him).
He will serve lunch.	Lunch will be served (by him).
He should serve lunch.	Lunch should be served (by him).

Irregular Verbs

Base form	Simple Past	Past Participle
awake	awoke	awoken
be	was	been
beat	beat	beat/beaten
become	became	become
begin	began	begun
bend	bent	bent
bid	bade/bid	bidden/bid
bite	bit	bitten/bit
bleed	bled	bled
blow	blew	blown

Base form	Simple Past	Past Participle
break	broke	broken
bring	brought	brought
build	built	built
burn	burned/burnt	burned/burnt
buy	bought	bought
catch	caught	caught
choose	chose	chosen
come	came	come
cost	cost	cost
cut	cut	cut
deal	dealt	dealt
dig	dug	dug
dive	dove/dived	dived
do	did	done
draw	drew	drawn
dream	dreamed/dreamt	dreamed/dreamt
drink	drank	drunk
eat	ate	eaten
fall	fell	fallen
feed	fed	fed
feel	felt	felt
fight	fought	fought
find	found	found
fly	flew	flown
forbid	forbade/forbad	forbidden

Reference Section

Base form	Simple Past	Past Participle
forget	forgot	forgotten
forgive	forgave	forgiven
freeze	froze	frozen
get	got	gotten/got
give	gave	given
go	went	gone
grow	grew	grown
hang	hung	hung
have	had	had
hear	heard	heard
hide	hid	hidden
hit	hit	hit
hold	held	held
hurt	hurt	hurt
keep	kept	kept
know	knew	known
lay	laid	laid
lead	led	led
learn	learned/learnt	learned/learnt
leave	left	left
lend	lent	lent
let	let	let
light	lit/lighted	lit/lighted
lose	lost	lost
make	made	made
meet	met	met

Base form	Simple Past	Past Participle
mistake	mistook	mistaken
pay	paid	paid
put	put	put
read	read	read
ride	rode	ridden
rise	rose	risen
run	ran	run
say	said	said
see	saw	seen
sell	sold	sold
send	sent	sent
shake	shook	shaken
shoot	shot	shot
shut	shut	shut
sing	sang	sung
sit	sat	sat
sleep	slept	slept
speak	spoke	spoken
speed	sped	sped
spend	spent	spent
spread	spread	spread
stand	stood	stood
steal	stole	stolen
stick	stuck	stuck
strike	struck	struck/stricken
swear	swore	sworn

Reference Section

Base form	Simple Past	Past Participle
swim	swam	swum
swing	swung	swung
take	took	taken
teach	taught	taught
tear	tore	torn
tell	told	told
think	thought	thought
throw	threw	thrown
understand	understood	understood
upset	upset	upset
wear	wore	worn
win	won	won
write	wrote	written

Imprimé sur Rolland Enviro®.
Ce papier contient 100% de fibres recyclées durables,
est fabriqué avec un procédé sans chlore
et à partir d'énergie biogaz.

www.ingramcontent.com/pod-product-compliance
Lightning Source LLC
Chambersburg PA
CBHW070846160426
43192CB00012B/2328